A QUESTION OF SPORT 4

COMPILED BY MIKE ADLEY

BBC BOOKS

Published by BBC Books,
a division of BBC Enterprises Ltd,
Woodlands, 80 Wood Lane, London W12 0TT

First published 1992

© BBC Enterprises Ltd 1992

ISBN 0 563 36407 6

Set in Times by Ace Filmsetting Ltd, Frome, Somerset
Printed and bound in England by Clays Ltd, St Ives plc
Colour separations by Dot Gradations Ltd, Chelmsford, Essex
Cover printed by Clays Ltd, St Ives plc

Picture Credits

All photographs supplied by Allsport Picture Agency with special thanks to
Tony Hicks. Except: Dave McAuley, Ginny Leng, Emlyn Hughes, Gareth
Edwards and page 8 © BBC; Brendan Foster UPP.

CONTENTS

INTRODUCTION

A Question of Sport is recorded on Sundays in BBC North's Studio A, the BBC's biggest studio outside London. Why Sundays, and why Manchester?

Manchester is where it all started in 1970 and only on a Sunday can you hope to pull together a collection of international sportspeople week after week. With their heavy training schedules and increasing travelling demands the fact that they give up their precious spare time for very little financial reward (everyone receives just the standard BBC fee) indicates the special place this simple programme holds in the affections of British sport.

Well, it might LOOK simple but, like clergymen, just because we perform on a Sunday doesn't mean we have the rest of the week off! There's an enormous amount of preparation by the production team between the fortnightly recordings. Even before one programme is 'in the can' work has started on the next and, because we like to record as close to transmission as possible, there is very little margin for error.

Finding the right mix of guests . . . locating suitable sporting clips, filming and carefully editing Mystery Personalities . . . and, of course, coming up with new questions, takes time, skill and sometimes a little luck!

My worst nightmare – of a guest ringing on Sunday to say they are injured or ill – doesn't happen often, but when it does it's a real panic to bring on a sub! So Sunday morning is a time for living on my nerves. David Coleman arrives around 9 o'clock after a 'crack of dawn' drive from his Buckinghamshire home. Unlike many quiz show hosts David wants to be involved with the programme all along the line, suggesting guests, sporting action and checking questions. He's already been studying the information we've sent by fax and video tape for several days. Sunday morning is when it all comes together – or not.

Most of the morning is spent in the studio with a run through for technicians, cameramen and the programme staff. Two teams of what we affectionately call 'Dummies' have been drafted in from local quiz leagues to play the part of the top sportspeople due that afternoon, David tries out his questions and his timings on them. After the rehearsal we discuss one or two changes which might make the afternoon recording better. Our backroom team set about re-editing the video tapes or finding additional information about an answer. David retires to his dressing room to give a final polish to his own notes. He is known in the business as the complete professional – anything less than 150% is an off day!

At around one o'clock the guests, their families and friends begin to arrive. We make a point of making this a family day out. Some of the best friendships in British sport have been forged by *A Question of Sport* – and it's not just the contestants. Their wives, girlfriends, husbands and children all enjoy meeting each other.

Then we all sit down in the BBC canteen for a traditional Sunday lunch of roast beef and yorkshire pudding. It's a great way of getting everyone to relax, have a laugh and prepare to face the nation on Britain's longest-running television quiz show.

Of course, we can't relax until the cameras stop rolling at around six o'clock that evening. Then there's the chance of a couple of drinks and I tell the team not to worry about the next programme . . . until tomorrow morning.

Mike Adley
Executive Producer *A Question of Sport* BBC NORTH

A QUESTION OF SPORT: THE FACTS

Twenty things you always wanted to know about the programme

1 The first programme was made in a deconsecrated Manchester church in January 1970. It went out in black and white and attracted 8.5 million viewers.

2 Soccer legends Tom Finney and George Best met for the first time when they were guests on the original programme.

3 Henry Cooper and Cliff Morgan were the original team captains. They stayed together for five years. Freddie Trueman took over from Cliff in 1976, followed by Brendan Foster in 1977.

4 Current captains Bill Beaumont and Ian Botham were still students when the programme started. Ian at school in Yeovil, Bill at Salford Technical College in Manchester.

5 Bill Beaumont holds the record for the number of appearances. In 10 years as captain he has clocked up over 200. In two spells as captain Emlyn Hughes only managed 122 programmes.

6 HRH The Princess Royal became the first member of the Royal Family to appear on a television quiz show when she was a guest in 1987. Over 18 million viewers saw Princess Anne jokingly threaten Emlyn Hughes with her handbag!

7 Despite its success the programme was 'rested' in 1978, so there have been only 21 series in 22 years.

8 David Vine was the original questionmaster. David Coleman took over in 1979 and introduced the 'friendly rivalry' style which continues to be so popular with viewers.

9 The programmes are still recorded in Manchester on Sunday afternoons. Guests and their families are invited to a traditional Sunday lunch of roast beef and yorkshire pudding.

10 None of the guests or captains know any of the questions beforehand. The only rehearsal goes on behind closed doors with members of local quiz leagues playing the parts of top sporting celebrities.

11 Being asked to appear is still seen as an honour. Many stars – or their agents – ring up and say 'when are we on?' The answer is usually 'When you've won something!'

12 Tickets for the recordings are like gold dust. There was once a three-year waiting list for tickets. But so far this is one top sporting event the touts have not moved in on.

13 No sportsperson can appear as a guest more than once a series. Showjumper Lucinda Green holds the record. Her appearance in February 1991 was her 15th.

14 What happened next? is the most popular item with contestants and viewers. Production staff scour the world's television to find suitable moments of sporting madness.

15 Research shows that over half of the viewers are women. Bill Beaumont receives the most fan mail from female viewers.

16 The average weekly audience of around 11 million would fill Wembley Stadium, Lord's Cricket Ground and the Wimbledon Centre Court 100 times over!

17 Questionmaster David Coleman claims to be the first person to appear in television's top ten on both BBC and ITV at the same time – on BBC with *A Question of Sport* and on ITV in *Spitting Image*.

18 No guests can ever be asked the same question twice. The computer in the *A Question of Sport* office keeps a record of 'who's had what and when'.

19 It's estimated that over 800 of the world's top sportsmen and women have been on the show. The number of refusals to appear doesn't even reach double figures.

20 *A Question of Sport* is Britain's longest-running television quiz. It has been on longer than *EastEnders*, *Neighbours*, and *Brookside* put together!

David, Ian and Bill . . .

DAVID COLEMAN

Sporting qualifications: As a young county standard athlete won the Manchester Mile in 1949. Played soccer for Stockport County Reserves.

A Question of Sport-ing Qualifications: Sports broadcaster for the BBC since 1951. Presented *Grandstand, Sportsnight with Coleman* and has commentated at 16 Olympic Games (Summer and Winter) since 1960. David says: 'Sport is big business nowadays, but I still believe it should be fun. That's why *A Question of Sport* just runs and runs. People enjoy seeing sporting personalities in a different light than on the playing field. Long may it continue.'

IAN BOTHAM

Sporting qualifications: An 18-year career as a county cricketer with Somerset, Worcestershire and now Durham. Played football for Scunthorpe United. Over 100 Test Matches and 100 One Day Internationals for England.

A Question of Sport-ing qualifications: Ian says: 'Millions of hours in hotel rooms all over the world watching sport on television because there was nothing else to do. Interest in golf, soccer . . . but I still hate cricket questions!'

BILL BEAUMONT

Sporting qualifications: Played a record 33 successive internationals for England and also captained his country on a record 21 occasions. Led England to the Grand Slam in 1980. Career cut short by injury in 1982.

A Question of Sport-ing qualifications: Bill says: 'I read the *Daily Telegraph* sports pages in my lunch hour every day, keep in touch with my old rugby mates and, after over 200 appearances on the programme, there can't be many questions I haven't heard!

GAME 1

In this game there is a guest from each of the home countries. Ian leads England and Wales, while Bill leads Ireland and Scotland.

BILL'S TEAM

DAVE McAULEY In September 1991 Dave set a new British post-war record by successfully defending his IBF world flyweight title for the fifth successive time. Before his ten-round victory over the diminutive South African Jake Matlala Dave had shared the record with Jim Watt. Dave had won the title for the first time in June 1989 by defeating Londoner Duke McKenzie after two unsuccessful shots against the Colombian Fidel Bassa.

YVONNE MURRAY This quietly spoken Scot from Musselburgh became Britain's only female gold medallist at the European Championships in Split by winning the 3000 metres. Such feats do not help Ian's memory for names, especially Scottish ones, which are usually forgotten in the time it takes him to down a celebratory pint after scoring one of his famous centuries against the Australians – just ask John Jeffrey or Liz McColgan!

IAN'S TEAM

DAVID PLATT made his League debut with Crewe Alexandra in the 1984–85 season, scoring 55 goals in 134 appearances. In 1987 he joined Aston Villa. His international debut for England came in November 1989, against Italy at Wembley. David's success in the 1990 World Cup Finals set him up for a lucrative transfer from Aston Villa to Bari in the Italian league. He was voted the PFA player of the year in 1990.

PAUL THORBURN During his long and distinguished career, the Welsh fullback has captained his club (Neath) and country. 'The Boot', as we call him, holds the record for the longest conversion in international rugby union, 70 yards. In 1991, against France, he passed the magic 300-point tally for place kicks. In the 1989–90 season Paul led Neath to victory in the Club Championship, the Welsh Challenge Cup and the Merit Table.

9

GAME 1
Pictureboard

1

2

3

4

?

GAME 1
Home & Away

DAVE
Who did Barry McGuigan defeat on 8 June 1985 to win the WBA World Featherweight title?

DAVID
Who scored 28 Cup and League goals to become the First Division's leading goalscorer in the 1989–90 season?

YVONNE
Who won both the world and European indoor 3000m titles in 1989?

PAUL
Name the only Welshman to score a Test match try on the British Lions' 1990 tour to Australia.

BILL
Name the venue for the last final of the English County championship before the event was moved to Twickenham in 1984.

IAN
Whose 299 runs in the second innings of the first Test against Sri Lanka in 1991 set a new record for the highest total ever scored for his country in a Test innings?

Horseracing: Why do the start times at Ireland's Laytown races vary according to the phase of the moon?

Tennis: Which American won both the men's and mixed doubles titles at Wimbledon in 1990?

Soccer: Who is the oldest man ever to captain a World Cup winning team?

Bowls: Name the 15-year-old lad from Reading who with his dad reached the semi-finals of the EBA National Pairs competition in 1990.

Cricket: Who notched up a famous double of 1000 Test match runs and 100 Test match wickets at Edgbaston in 1990?

Showjumping: Who was the only rider to win three successive Hickstead Derbies in the 1980s?

GAME 1
One-Minute Round

1 (1 pt)   Boxing: Who was the first Briton to win a world title three times at the same weight?

2 (1 pt)   Athletics: Name the woman who set a new Olympic record for the 1500m in Seoul.

3 (2 pts) Ice Hockey: The 1991 Stanley Cup was contested between the North Stars and the Penguins. Which North American cities do they represent?

4 (1 pt)   Tennis: Who ended Steffi Graf's 66-match winning streak at the 1990 German Open?

5 (1 pt)   Horseracing: Only one horse has won the Oaks at odds of 50–1 this century. Who was she?

6 (3 pts) Each of these personalities shares his surname with a First Division club. Name them.
a) Soccer: Alan (?)
b) Snooker: Clive (?)
c) Rugby: Andrew (?)

1 (1 pt)   Soccer: Which team spoilt Liverpool's 100 per cent home record at Anfield in 1989?

2 (1 pt)   Cycling: Which rider notched up his third Tour de France victory in 1990?

3 (2 pts)   American Football: Which two teams each contested successive Superbowl finals in the 1980s?

4 (1 pt)   Rugby Union: Name the first player to score 600 points in international rugby.

5 (1 pt)   Golf: Which Australian won the US PGA at Shoal Creek in 1990?

6 (3 pts)   The missing names are all school lessons!
        a) Cricket: Bruce (?)
        b) Soccer: Tommy (?)
        c) Golf: (?) Wall.

GAME 1
Mystery Personality

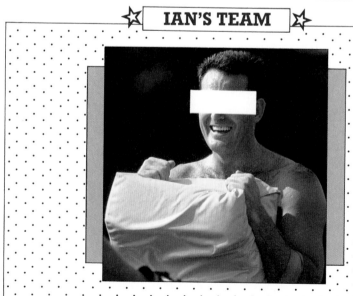

GAME 1 ANSWERS

PICTUREBOARD

1 **Erik Thorstvedt:** Spurs' Norwegian international goalkeeper in action.
2 **Sandra Farmer-Patrick:** Winning the 400m at the New York Grand Prix meeting, 1991.
3 **Bonnie Blair:** US Olympic gold medallist speedskating superstar.
4 **Jeremy Guscott:** One of England's Rugby World Cup heroes in 1991.

HOME & AWAY

DAVE (HOME)
Eusebio Pedroza. McGuigan ended Pedroza's seven-year reign as world champion at Loftus Road.

(AWAY)
Because the races are held on a beach and the tides are dictated by the phase of the moon. The races are held annually during the last week in August. Laytown is 27 miles north of Dublin and the meeting is under the rules of the Irish Jockey Club.

DAVID (HOME)
John Barnes of Liverpool. He scored 22 in the League, 5 in the FA Cup and 1 in the League Cup. Gary Lineker scored 24 League goals but just two in Cup competitions.

(AWAY)
Rick Leach. He won the men's title with Jim Pugh and the mixed doubles with Zina Garrison.

YVONNE (HOME)
Ellie Van Holst. She successfully defended her European title in 1990.

(AWAY)
Dino Zoff. Aged 40 he captained the Italian side which beat West Germany 3–1 in the final in Madrid in 1982. Zoff played 112 times for Italy between 1968 and 1983. He won a UEFA Cup winner's medal in 1977 with Juventus.

PAUL (HOME)
Ieuan Evans, whose try secured a 19 points to 18 win and the Lions' first Test series victory in Australia for 15 years. The Lions won the series 2–1.

(AWAY)
Robert Newman. He and his father Mike were beaten 20 points to 18 by the eventual champions John Ottaway and Roger Guy. They also reached the quarter-finals of the triples.

15

BILL (HOME)
Bristol. Gloucestershire beat Yorkshire by 19 points to 7. Gloucestershire retained the title in 1984, beating Somerset 36–18 at Twickenham.

(AWAY)
John Bracewell of New Zealand, in the Third Test and, incredibly, on the same day. He became only the second New Zealander in history to pull off this double; the first was Sir Richard Hadlee.

IAN (HOME)
Martin Crowe, for New Zealand in Wellington where the match was drawn. His runs also contributed to a world record third-wicket partnership of 467 with Andrew Jones, who scored 186. Martin Crowe was at Somerset with Ian.

(AWAY)
Nick Skelton. He won his first Derby, in 1987, on Raffles, his second in 1988 on Apollo, and his third on Burmah Apollo.

ONE-MINUTE ROUND

BILL'S TEAM
1 Dennis Andries at light heavyweight, winning the title in 1986 and regaining it in 1989 and 1990.
2 Paula Ivan (Romania).
3 Minnesota (North Stars), Pittsburgh (Penguins). The Penguins were the eventual winners.
4 Monica Seles.
5 Jet Ski Lady.
6 a) Sunderland b) Everton c) Leeds.

IAN'S TEAM
1 Coventry, by winning 1–0 with a goal from Cyrille Regis.
2 Greg Lemond (USA), to join that select band of Laurie Fignon, Bernard Hinault, Eddy Merckx, Jacques Anquetil and Louison Bobet.
3 Denver Broncos 87–88; Washington Redskins 83–84.
4 Michael Lynagh (Australia), passed 600 points in 1991, and is still going.
5 Wayne Grady, beating Fred Couples by three shots.
6 a) French b) English c) Art.

MYSTERY PERSONALITY

BILL'S TEAM   Monica Seles: Yugoslavian tennis sensation, US Open, 1991.

IAN'S TEAM   David Campese: in training for Australia's Rugby World Cup campaign, 1991.

GAME 2

The speed and agility of Colin Jackson coupled with the strength and size of John Jeffrey should give Ian an advantage. Bill lines up with two of the best known and most knowledgeable racing experts ever invited into the *A Question of Sport* studio, John Parrott and Bryan Robson.

☆ IAN'S TEAM ☆

COLIN JACKSON Colin burst onto the world stage by winning the gold medal at the World Junior Championships in 1986. He became only the third man in history to break 13 seconds. His battles with America's Roger Kingdom and now Britain's Tony Jarrett have brought the 110m hurdles a new popularity in this country and thrilled tv audiences around the world.

JOHN JEFFREY How could Ian fail to recognise one of rugby union's best known faces, especially as he purports to be an avid follower and knows a thing or two about the sport? It happened when the Kelso wingforward made one of his regular appearances on the Pictureboard. Ian remembered that John was a potato farmer in the Borders. He even recalled that John had led his club to the championship, and that he was a member of Scotland's grand slam-winning side of 1990. But, he could not remember his name. J.J. will certainly not let him forget it tonight.

☆ BILL'S TEAM ☆

JOHN PARROTT With Arsenal winning the League and Spurs the Cup, John was determined that Merseyside should have a major trophy in 1991. So, showing the good form he had for years reserved for the World Snooker Championship, he defeated Steve Davis in the semi-finals and stormed into a 6–0 lead in the final against the 'whirlwind' Jimmy White. By the final Monday of the tournament he had won the world title and given his beloved Merseyside their major trophy.

BRYAN ROBSON The many battles with Everton or Liverpool in both Cup and League will be forgotten as Bryan joins forces with John Parrott. Their common interest, horseracing, will dominate the conversation. Bryan has won international honours at all levels with England, leading them to two World Cup finals. His record with Manchester United is just as impressive, captaining them to three FA Cup final victories.

17

Pictureboard

1

2

3

4

?

GAME 2
Home & Away

COLIN
In 1928, Sydney Atkinson of South Africa became the first non-American to win the Olympic 110m hurdles title. Can you name the second non-American to win the same title?

JOHN (PARROTT)
Television commentator Jimmy Meadowcroft hit the headlines because his opponent recorded a maximum in the first round of the 1988 European Open at Blackpool. Who was he?

JOHN (JEFFREY)
Name the brothers who played in grand slam-winning sides for Scotland, one in 1984, the other in 1990.

BRYAN
Name the last man to score in Manchester and Merseyside derbies in successive years.

IAN
Which batsman hit Eddie Hemmings for four successive Test match sixes at Lord's?

BILL
Who scored two tries on his England debut against Ireland at Twickenham in 1986?

When leaving the Swiss Bank and travelling towards Highway 89 you will pass both Amen and Moonshine, but what would you be doing?

Horseracing: Name the Irish jockey who won Classics in England, Ireland and France in 1990.

Soccer: The last Welshman to captain an FA Cup-winning side did so in 1984. Who was he?

Rugby League: Which team reached three successive premiership finals in the 1980s, losing on each occasion?

Swimming: Name the European who won his thirteenth world championship medal in 1990.

The only woman to win a world championship rally in motor sport did so in Brazil in 1982. Who was she?

GAME 2
One-Minute Round

1 (1 pt) Golf: Name the last course to stage the British Open championship for the first time.

2 (1 pt) Motor Racing: Where did Riccardo Patrese achieve his only Formula One Grand Prix win in 1990?

3 (2 pts) Athletics: Name the winners of the Olympic 110m hurdles title in the 1980s.

4 (1 pt) Rugby Union: The only Scot to score a brace of tries in the 1989–90 Home International season did so against Ireland. Name him.

5 (1 pt) Golf: Who was the last American to successfully defend the US Masters title?

6 (3 pts) The following share their names with religious people:
   a) Cricket: Mark (?)
   b) Soccer: Ian (?)
   c) Boxing: Michael (?)

1 (1 pt)   Snooker: Who lost two world championship finals in the 1980s?

2 (1 pt)   In which sport did Staffordshire's Phil Taylor win his first world title in 1990?

3 (2 pts)   Name the last city to twice play host to the Olympic Games.

4 (1 pt)   Soccer: Name England's captain at the 1982 World Cup Finals.

5 (1 pt)   Who was the only Australian to become the world 500cc motorcyling champion?

6 (3 pts)   These sportsmen share their names with precious stones:
   a) Soccer: Paul (?)
   b) Rugby League: Steve (?)
   c) Golf: (?) Young.

GAME 2
Mystery Personality

GAME 2 ANSWERS

PICTUREBOARD

1 **Phil Tufnell:** Middlesex and England spin bowler relaxes in Australia in 1991.
2 **Katrina Krabbe:** German sprinter in the blocks at the European Championships, 1990.
3 **Gianluca Vialli:** In action for Sampdoria v Napoli, 1991.
4 **Payne Stewart:** 1991 US Open Champion in action at the British Open, 1990.

HOME & AWAY

COLIN (HOME)
Guy Drut of France, who won gold in 1976 in Montreal with a time of 13.30 sec.

(AWAY)
Skiing. These are landmarks on the world championship downhill course at Vail-Beaver Creek in Colorado. The championships were held there in 1989. Highway 89 is a 'flat' about ⅓ of a mile long. The Swiss Bank is a high left-handed turn. Amen is a jump and Moonshine a section of ripples and rolls.

JOHN (PARROT) (HOME)
Alain Robidoux of Canada. Robidoux turned professional in 1988. It was not televised.

(AWAY)
Pat Eddery, who won the Derby on Quest For Fame, the Irish 2000 Guineas on Tirol, the French 1000 Guineas on House Proud and the French Derby on Sanglamore. Eddery was champion jockey on the Flat that season – his ninth title.

JOHN (JEFFREY) (HOME)
Jim and Finlay Calder. Jim won 27 caps, Finlay 28.

(AWAY)
Kevin Ratcliffe of Everton. Everton beat Watford 2–0 on the day, with goals from Graeme Sharp and Andy Gray.

BRYAN (HOME)
Andy Hinchcliffe. He scored for Manchester City against United in 1990 and for Everton against Liverpool the following season.

(AWAY)
Hull. Hull Kingston Rovers defeated them in 1981, Widnes in 1982 and 1983.

IAN (HOME)
Kapil Dev. He achieved the feat in the First Test against England in 1990, enabling India to save the follow on. It was the first time any player had hit four successive sixes in a Test. In this Test Graham Gooch scored a memorable 333.

(AWAY)
Michael Gross of Germany. At the world championships in Perth, he won a gold in the 4×200m freestyle, two individual silvers, and a bronze in the medley relay. His medal tally also includes four individual titles in 1982 and 1986.

BILL (HOME)
Dean Richards. England beat Ireland 25 points to 20.

(AWAY)
Michelle Mouton of France.

ONE-MINUTE ROUND

IAN'S TEAM
1 Turnberry (1977).
2 San Marino.
3 Thomas Munkelt, 1980; Roger Kingdom, 1984 and 1988.
4 Derek White.
5 Jack Nicklaus, in 1965 and 1966.
6 a) Priest   b) Bishop   c) Nunn.

BILL'S TEAM
1 Steve Davis: to Dennis Taylor in 1985 and Joe Johnson in 1986.
2 Darts. He won it again in 1992.
3 Los Angeles, in 1932 and 1984.
4 Mick Mills of Ipswich.
5 Wayne Gardner, in 1987.
6 a) Jewell   b) Diamond   c) Sapphire.

MYSTERY PERSONALITY

IAN'S TEAM   Jim Courier: US tennis star, Paris, 1991.

BILL'S TEAM   Ian Wright: Arsenal and England striker.

GAME 3

With the big guns joining both Bill and Ian we are guaranteed plenty of noise – Ginny Leng lines up with Bill and the Liverpool captain Ronnie Whelan, while Kriss Akabusi is alongside Ian and Gavin Hastings.

☆ BILL'S TEAM ☆

GINNY LENG A combination of superb horsemanship and strength of character took Ginny to a hat-trick of European individual titles in the 1980s; with Priceless in 1985, Night Cap in 1987 and Master Craftsman in 1989. In 1986 she reached the zenith of her career, becoming world champion, again with Priceless. Ginny's presence tonight should guarantee a rider or two on the Pictureboard and Bill at least a couple of welcome points.

RONNIE WHELAN The Liverpool and Republic of Ireland midfielder joined Liverpool in 1981. During the course of some 300 games in the 1980s he won five League Championship medals, two FA Cup medals, three League Cup medals and was in the Liverpool side that won the European Cup in 1984. He rounded off the decade in style by leading Liverpool to victory in the FA Cup against the old enemy, Everton.

☆ IAN'S TEAM ☆

KRISS AKABUSI The former warrant officer in the British Army has had a couple of opportunities to fine tune his vocal cords on this programme. A member of Team Solent, Kriss is the Commonwealth and European 400m hurdles champion. He returned home from the 1991 World Championships with a bronze medal for the hurdles and the admiration of the world for his final leg in the 4×400m relay. This was one of the few occasions when Kriss was rendered speechless.

GAVIN HASTINGS The London Scottish full-back seems to break a Scottish record every time he dons the dark blue jumper. He won his first cap in the 1985–86 season, converting 14 penalty goals in the international championship that season, a new Scottish record. In 1987 he scored a record 27 points against Romania. He was a member of the grand slam-winning side of 1990. Ian will be hoping that a record score tonight will put him on the winning side.

GAME 3
Pictureboard

1

2

3

4

?

GAME 3
Home & Away

GINNY
Who was the only man to win Burghley twice in the 1980s?

KRISS
Who won the 400m hurdles Olympic gold medal in 1972 in a time which stood as the Commonwealth record until the 1991 World Championships, when it was broken by Samuel Matete of Zambia?

RONNIE
Which current First Division manager and his son have both played international football for England?

GAVIN
Name the brothers who won Welsh international caps in the same year, one against the All Blacks, the other against the Barbarians.

BILL
Who on his English debut created a new international points-scoring record by kicking eight conversions?

IAN
Which Australian took a hat-trick of wickets against the West Indies in 1989 with deliveries in three different overs?

Rugby Union: Which player has scored most points for the British Lions in Tests?

Cricket: Whose 'duck' in the Second Test at Melbourne in 1990 ended a record run of 119 Test innings without such a failure?

Horseracing: Which jockey rode his mount to second place in the Grand National three times between 1986 and 1990?

Athletics: The winner of the gold medal for Canada in the 3000m steeplechase at the Commonwealth Games in 1986 had previously won the silver for England in 1982. Who was he?

Squash: Which Australian woman won four successive British Open titles in the 1980s?

In which sport would you find a goose-egg, a mackerel, and ducks on the pond?

GAME 3
One-Minute Round

1 (1 pt) Soccer: Who scored the winning goal in the 1990 Cup final replay, defeating Crystal Palace?

2 (1 pt) Eventing: Who won a European title on Mystic Minstre

3 (2 pts) Tennis: Which Czechoslovak pair won the 1990 Australian Women's Open doubles title?

4 (1 pt) With which sport do you associate Toni Nieminen?

5 (1 pt) Golf: On which course did Tom Watson win his first British Open title?

6 (3 pts) Their namesakes are all famous detectives:
   a) Swimming: Catherine (?)
   b) Soccer: Roy (?)
   c) Rowing: Andy (?)

1 (1 pt)   Rugby Union: Who is Scotland's most capped full-back?

2 (1 pt)   Motor Racing: Which driver won the British Grand Prix three times in the 1980s?

3 (2 pts)   Snooker: Who defeated Steve Davis to reach the 1990 Rothmans Grand Prix Final?

4 (1 pt)   Athletics: Name the only country to have had four Olympic 3000m steeplechase champions since 1968.

5 (1 pt)   Tennis: Who ended Steffi Graf's bid for a hat-trick of Wimbledon singles titles by beating her in the semis?

6 (3 pts)   The following names will be found on a calendar:
a) Archery: (?) Moon.
b) Athletics: (?) Uti.
c) Boxing: Bernd (?)

GAME 3
Mystery Personality

GAME 3 ANSWERS

PICTUREBOARD

1 **Leroy Burrell:** Former 100m World record holder doing the high jump in his blocks, Cologne, 1990.

2 **John Whittaker:** On Henderson Milton in the World Equestrian Games, 1990.

3 **Mary Jo Fernandez:** US tennis star wiping her brow, Pilkington Glass tournament in 1991.

4 **Mike Atherton:** Dodging a delivery, 3rd Test v Australia, Sydney, 1991.

HOME & AWAY

GINNY (HOME)
Richard Walker (GB). Walker won in 1980 on John of Gaunt, and in 1982 on Ryan's Cross. Mark Todd won in 1987 and in 1990. No other man won the title in that period.

(AWAY)
Phil Bennett. He scored 44 points for the Lions in eight appearances between 1974 and 1977. He is the Lions' most capped fly-half.

KRISS (HOME)
John Akii-Bua of Uganda in 47.82 sec. Matete's run in 1991 was clocked at 47.64 sec, Kriss himself got the bronze. Kriss also won the European title with 47.92 sec to break David Hemery's UK record (48.12), set in the 1968 Olympics.

(AWAY)
David Gower's. Gower was caught by Border off Greg Matthews in the second innings, having scored 100 in the first innings. His previous Test 'duck' came against Pakistan at Lord's in 1982.

RONNIE (HOME)
Brian and Nigel Clough. Brian played twice for England while with Middlesbrough.

(AWAY)
Chris Grant, on Durham Edition in 1990 at 9–1 and 1988 at 20–1; on Young Driver in 1986 at 66–1.

GAVIN (HOME)
Glyn and Gareth Llewellyn. Both play for Neath.

(AWAY)
Graham Fell. He took the gold in Edinburgh in 1986, the silver four years earlier in Brisbane behind Julius Korir of Kenya. Fell was born in Romford, Essex, and studied at Nottingham University.

BILL (HOME)
Simon Hodgkinson of Nottingham, in a 58–3 victory against Romania in 1989.

(AWAY)
Vicky Hoffman (now Cardwell).

IAN (HOME)
Merv Hughes, in the Second Test in Perth. Hughes dismissed Curtley Ambrose with the last ball of his 36th over, then picked up the wicket of Patrick Patterson with the first ball of his 37th over to end the West Indies' first innings. With the first ball of his first over in the second innings, he dismissed Gordon Greenidge. He took thirteen wickets in the match!

(AWAY)
Baseball. A goose-egg describes an innings in which no runs have been scored, ducks on the pond arise when all the bases are loaded, and a mackerel is a curving delivery or 'curveball'.

ONE-MINUTE ROUND

BILL'S TEAM
1 Lee Martin of Manchester United.
2 Rachel Bayliss, in 1983.
3 Helena Sukova and Jana Novotna.
4 Ski-jumping.
5 Carnoustie, in 1975.
6 a) Poirot   b) Ironside   c) Holmes.

IAN'S TEAM
1 Andy Irvine; 47 caps at full-back and 4 caps as a winger, 51 in total.
2 Alain Prost, in 1983, 1985 and 1989.
3 Nigel Bond; he lost in the final to Stephen Hendry.
4 Kenya.
5 Zina Garrison, in 1990.
6 a) April   b) Sunday   c) August.

MYSTERY PERSONALITY

BILL'S TEAM   Chris Woods: England goalkeeper, now with Sheffield Wednesday, in action for Rangers v Celtic, 1991.

IAN'S TEAM   Surya Bonaly: French star of figure skating.

GAME 4

In this game, Ian's gone for youth in the form of Matthew Le Tissier and experience with friend and hero Ian Woosnam. Bill's choice of Angus Fraser should increase the pressure on Ian to answer his cricket questions correctly. Bill and Angus are joined by the athlete Roger Black.

☆ IAN'S TEAM ☆

MATTHEW LE TISSIER Young players have a lot to lose on this show – one mistake and they suffer the consequences in the dressing rooms from team mates, and on the terraces from the fans. These worries did not deter Guernsey's soccer hero Matthew Le Tissier, PFA Young Player of the Year in 1990, from taking his place alongside Ian. His experiences in the first division with Southampton and at international level with England B should keep this team well balanced tonight.

IAN WOOSNAM The 1991 US Masters champion will have spent most of the summer on the US tour so the chances of his spotting us filming Mystery Personalities have been reduced. On two previous appearances he has had the incredible luck of being asked to identify sequences of clips which he saw us filming. With breaks of over 50 at snooker and a keen love of fishing, Ian will have plenty to discuss with his captain tonight.

☆ BILL'S TEAM ☆

ANGUS FRASER If Bill had any doubts about this young fast bowler from Middlesex they were soon dispelled when he found out that Angus is a fellow Lancastrian, born at Billinge in August 1965, and a Liverpool supporter. Angus made his Test debut for England in the 1989 series against Australia and celebrated by taking four wickets in the first innings. Against India the following year he topped the bowling averages with 16 wickets at an average of 28.75 runs.

ROGER BLACK Roger hit the headlines in 1986 by winning individual and relay gold medals at both the European Championships and Commonwealth Games. In 1988 an ankle injury threatened his career, but in 1990 he successfully defended both titles at Split. He was a member of the $4 \times 400m$ relay team that won the gold medal in the world championships in Tokyo. Away from the track, Roger is a Southampton fan, enjoys tennis and plays the guitar.

GAME 4
Pictureboard

1

2

3

4

?

GAME 4
Home & Away

MATTHEW
Which nation ended England's six-year unbeaten run with a 2–1 victory at Wembley in May 1990?

If you are in a race in which the Devil Takes the Hindmost, what are you doing?

ANGUS
Which Australian bowler took 83 English Test wickets in the 1980s?

Waterskiing: Name the woman who successfully defended her overall world title in 1989.

IAN
Name the defending Open champion who failed to make the cut at St Andrews in 1990.

Snooker: Who brought Stephen Hendry's reign as world champion to an end in 1991?

ROGER
The winner of the Commonwealth Games 400m in 1982 went on to take the gold at the first world championships a year later. Who was he?

Horseracing: On which horse did Dick Saunders win the 1982 Grand National?

IAN
Two players scored more than one century during the 1989–90 West Indies v England Test series. Allan Lamb was one. Can you name the other?

Who set a Five Nations' record in 1983 by scoring a total of 52 points?

BILL
England conceded just three tries in the 1989–90 Five Nations' Championship. Lagisquet scored one for France and Stanger for Scotland. Who scored the other?

Name the only man to lift the FA Cup in successive years during the 1980s.

GAME 4
One-Minute Round

1 (1 pt) Horseracing: Willie Carson rode Salsabil to victory in two Classics. The Oaks was one. Can you name the other?

2 (1 pt) Who did Pete Sampras defeat in the 1990 US Open singles final?

3 (2 pts) Snooker: Name the players who contested the first world championship final at the Crucible Theatre?

4 (1 pt) Tennis: Who partnered Jo Durie to her Wimbledon mixed doubles title?

5 (1 pt) Golf: Who captained Europe's 1991 Ryder Cup team?

6 (3 pts) The following share their names with American Presidents:
   a) Boxing: (?) McKinney.
   b) Athletics: (?) Jackson.
   c) Skiing: Bill (?).

1 (1 pt) Cricket: Which county lost both one-day finals at Lord's in 1987?

2 (1 pt) Golf: Who was the first Briton to win the World Matchplay title twice?

3 (2 pts) Soccer: Everton were the runners–up in successive FA Cup finals during the 1980s. Who were the winners?

4 (1 pt) Athletics: Which Australian won Commonwealth gold medals at 100, 200 and 400 metres?

5 (1 pt) Showjumping: Name the woman who won the world title in 1986.

6 (3 pts) These sportsmen share their names with British Prime Ministers:
a) Athletics: (?) Mahorn.
b) Soccer: Nigel (?)
c) Cricket: (?) Small.

GAME 4
Mystery Personality

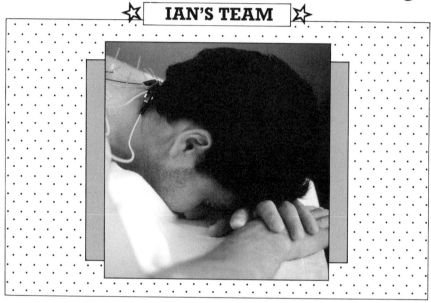

GAME 4 ANSWERS

PICTUREBOARD

1 **Heike Heinkel:** Germany's star high jumper.
2 **Ruud Gullit:** Soccer genius of AC Milan and Holland.
3 **John Daly:** US PGA Champion, 1991.
4 **Steve Watkin:** Glamorgan and England pace bowler.

HOME & AWAY

MATTHEW (HOME)
Uruguay. England's previous defeat was against the Soviet Union (2–0) in June 1984.

(AWAY)
Cycling: 'The Devil Takes the Hindmost' is an elimination race in which a field is whittled down to the two riders who will contest the final sprint. The last man to cross the finishing line at the end of each lap is eliminated.

ANGUS (HOME)
Terry Alderman. He took 42 wickets in the 1981 series, 41 wickets in the 1989 series.

(AWAY)
Deenah Brush-Mapple of the USA. She is married to Britain's Andy Mapple, who won the world slalom title in 1989.

IAN (HOME)
Mark Calcavecchia, with a two-round total of 146. He also missed the cut in the US Open and US PGA that year. Tom Watson was the last champion to miss the cut at the Open, in 1976.

(AWAY)
Steve James, by beating him 13–11 in the quarter-final.

ROGER (HOME)
Bert Cameron. He won the Commonwealth gold in Brisbane in 45.89 sec, and the world title in 43.05. Roger Black succeeded Cameron as Commonwealth champion in 1986.

(AWAY)
Grittar. Saunders became the fifth amateur jockey to win the race since the Second World War when he brought the 7–1 shot home.

IAN (HOME)
Desmond Haynes. Lamb scored 132 in the First Test and 119 in the Fourth. Haynes scored 109 in the Fourth Test and 167 in the Fifth Test. England lost the series 2–1.

(AWAY)
Ollie Campbell. He set a record of 46 points in 1980, which he equalled in 1982. Lescarboura beat Ollie's 1983 record in 1984 with 54 points.

BILL (HOME)
Phil Davies of Wales. England finished runners-up to Scotland after a memorable grand slam decider at Murrayfield.

(AWAY)
Steve Perryman of Tottenham. In 1981 Spurs beat Manchester City 3–2 after a replay, and in 1982 Steve and his team beat Queens Park Rangers 1–0, in yet another replay.

ONE-MINUTE ROUND

IAN'S TEAM
1 1000 Guineas.
2 Andre Agassi.
3 John Spencer and Cliff Thorburn in 1977; Spencer won.
4 Jeremy Bates, in 1987.
5 Bernard Gallagher. He played in eight successive Ryder Cup competitions between 1969 and 1983.
6 a) Kennedy   b) Roosevelt   c) Johnson.

BILL'S TEAM
1 Northants: the NatWest to Notts and the Benson and Hedges to Yorks.
2 Ian Woosnam, in 1987 and 1990.
3 Manchester United in 1985, Liverpool in 1986.
4 Raeleen Boyle, between 1970 and 1982.
5 Gail Greenhough of Canada, on Mr T.
6 a) Atlee   b) Callaghan of Aston Villa   c) Gladstone.

MYSTERY PERSONALITY

IAN'S TEAM   Jose Maria Olazabal: Spanish Ryder Cup player undergoing acupuncture for back pain, Japan, 1991.

BILL'S TEAM   John Parrott: Merseyside's favourite snooker player.

GAME 5

There is a true European flavour about this game. Bill is joined by Spain's Arantxa Sanchez and Ian by Italy's Frankie Dettori. England's international stars John Regis and Peter Beardsley make up the teams.

☆ BILL'S TEAM ☆

JOHN REGIS is the South London athlete who announced his arrival on the international scene in 1987 by winning the 200 metres bronze medal at the world championships in Rome. John, cousin of the Coventry City striker Cyrille, opened the 1990s with four medals at the European championships in Split, two gold medals in the 200m and 4×400m relay, a silver in the 4×100m relay and a bronze in the 100m. In 1991 he added to his collection, with a gold at the world championships in the 4×400m relay.

FRANKIE DETTORI is the son of Italian champion jockey Gianfranco, twice winner of the 2000 Guineas in the 1970s, Milan-born Lanfranco arrived at Newmarket in 1985 aged 15 as an apprentice to Luca Cumani. In 1989 he became the champion apprentice with 75 winners, equalling Eddie Hide's longstanding record. He says he's 'into' golf and that if there are any questions on soccer they had better be about the Italian League.

☆ IAN'S TEAM ☆

ARANTXA SANCHEZ VICARIO We expected the name Arantxa to give Ian a pronunciation problem, as it had to many tennis commentators when she first arrived on the scene. The tables were turned when the name of Ian Botham caused the biggest problem, as Arantxa insisted on calling him 'Iron Bottom'! In 1989 she became the youngest ever player to win the French Open Ladies' Singles title. She is the youngest in a family whose four children are all tennis professionals.

PETER BEARDSLEY joined Newcastle via Carlisle, Vancouver Whitecaps and Manchester United. He moved to Liverpool for £1.9 million in 1987. With Liverpool he won two League championship medals and an FA Cup winner's medal. In the latter competition, Liverpool beat Everton, the club Peter was transferred to for £1.1 million in the summer of 1991. His active interest in snooker and cricket should assist Ian's team. Any horseracing questions will also be welcome.

GAME 5
Pictureboard

1

2

3

4

GAME 5
Home & Away

JOHN
Which Birchfield Harrier reached the Olympic 200m final in Seoul?

Rugby League: Which club provided a record 10 players for Great Britain in the 28-man squad to tour Papua New Guinea and New Zealand in 1990?

ARANTXA
Who won the 1990 French Ladies' Open title to become the youngest winner of a grand slam event this century?

Hockey: To which nation did Great Britain's ladies lose the bronze medal play-off at the 1988 Olympics in Seoul?

FRANKIE
Which jockey rode eight winners at Royal Ascot in 1989?

Where would you find the Coffins, Walkinshaw's Grave and Miss Granger's Bosoms?

PETER
Name the only player to lift the FA Cup on three occasions with the same team.

Where are Goddards and Craner Curves found?

BILL
Who in 1990 completed a unique family hat-trick, following both his father and grandfather, by representing his country in the Five Nations' championship?

Name the Briton who defeated Rolando Bohol to win the IBF World Flyweight title at Wembley in 1988.

IAN
Whose 366 against Surrey was the highest first class innings of the 1990 English season?

Soccer: Name the first Scottish side to reach the final of the UEFA Cup.

GAME 5

One-Minute Round

1 (1 pt)   Athletics: Name the country that set a new world record in Split for the men's 4 × 100m relay.

2 (1 pt)   Horseracing: Who rode Tirol to victory in the 2000 Guineas?

3 (1 pt)   Golf: On which English course did Tom Watson win his only Open title?

4 (2 pts)   Athletics: Name two of the three Americans who won medals in the 400m at the 1988 Olympics.

5 (1 pt)   Tennis: Which man reached two grand slam finals in 1990, losing both?

6 (3 pts)   All these missing names will be found on *The Magic Roundabout*:
     a)   Athletics: (?) Griffith-Joyner
     b)   Soccer: Kevin (?)
     c)   Motor Racing: Rad (?)

1 (1 pt)   Tennis: Name the only woman to win four United States Open titles in the 1980s.

2 (1 pt)   Horseracing: How many Classics did Lester Piggott win before his first retirement?

3 (2 pts) Name the last two cities to stage the Spanish Grand Prix.

4 (1 pt)   Soccer: Which was the last English team to retain the European Cup?

5 (1 pt)   Athletics: Which Commonwealth Games 400m champion played rugby league with Balmain?

6 (3 pts) These missing names are all weather conditions:
a) Motor Cycling: Wayne (?)
b) Boxing: Jimmy (?)
c) Golf: David (?)

Mystery Personality

GAME 5 ANSWERS

PICTUREBOARD

1 **Nelson Piquet:** Contemplating no points won at the San Marino Grand Prix in 1991.
2 **Gordon Strachan:** In action for Leeds v Manchester United. Lee Sharp is grounded.
3 **Anke Huber:** Future star of German tennis.
4 **Mike Powell:** Holder of the World Long Jump Record, set in 1991.

HOME & AWAY

JOHN (HOME)
Michael Rosswess. He finished seventh. Linford Christie narrowly missed out on the medals, finishing fourth behind Joe de Loach, Carl Lewis and Robson da Silva.

(AWAY)
Wigan. Ellery Hanley, the skipper, was forced to withdraw due to an ankle injury before the tour began, reducing Wigan's representation to nine.

ARANTXA (HOME)
Monica Seles of Yugoslavia. Seles was 16 years and 6 months old when she beat Steffi Graf in the final of the French. Lottie Dodd was just 15 years and 10 months when she won Wimbledon in 1887. Arantxa won the French title in 1989 aged 17 years and 5 months.

(AWAY)
Holland. Britain lost 3–1, Mary Nevill scoring their only goal. Australia took the gold and Korea, the host nation, the silver.

FRANKIE (HOME)
Pat Eddery. Despite this feat, Dettori was named jockey of the month (June), with 20 winners.

(AWAY)
St Andrews, the Old Course. The Coffins are bunkers on the sixth and thirteenth. Walkinshaw's Grave is a bunker named after Mr Walkinshaw, a 19th-century golfer who regularly topped his ball off the sixth tee into this bunker. Miss Granger was a lady member after whom two bunkers on the fifteenth were named. These have now been renamed the Himalayas.

PETER (HOME)
Bryan Robson. He captained
Manchester United to victories
against Brighton in 1983, Everton
in 1985 and Crystal Palace in 1990.

(AWAY)
Donnington Park. The track
currently hosts the British
Motorcycling Grand Prix.

BILL (HOME)
Kenny Murphy, the Cork
Constitution full-back. He made
his debut against England in 1990.
His father Noel won 41 caps, while
Grandfather Noel Snr won 11.

(AWAY)
Duke McKenzie. After his
eleventh-round win, McKenzie
made one successful defence,
against Tony De Luca, before
Dave McAuley took his title in
June the following year.

IAN (HOME)
Neil Fairbrother. His triple century
was one of only three scored that
season. Jimmy Cook scored 313
not out for Somerset against
Glamorgan, and Graham Gooch
hit 333 for England against India.

(AWAY)
Dundee United, in 1987 against
Gothenburg. They lost 2–1 on
aggregate.

ONE-MINUTE ROUND

BILL'S TEAM
1 France, in a time of 37.79 sec.
2 Michael Kinane.
3 Royal Birkdale, in 1983.
4 Steve Lewis (gold), Butch Reynolds (silver) and Danny Everett (bronze).
5 Andre Agassi (USA). He lost both French and US Open finals.
6 a) Florence   b) Dillon   c) Dougall. Florence Griffith-Joyner won three
  gold medals at the Seoul Olympics. Kevin Dillon plays for Newcastle.
  Rad Dougall was a Formula Two racing driver in the late 1970s.

IAN'S TEAM
1 Martina Navratilova, in 1983, 1984, 1986 and 1987.
2 29, between 1954 and 1985, a record.
3 Jerez and Barcelona.
4 Nottingham Forest, in 1980.
5 Darren Clark.
6 a) Rainey   b) Thunder   c) Frost. Wayne Rainey was 1990 500cc world
  champion. Jimmy Thunder is a heavyweight boxer. South African David
  Frost plays on the US Tour.

MYSTERY PERSONALITY

BILL'S TEAM   Andre Agassi: unorthodox hero of American tennis.

IAN'S TEAM   Sergey Bubka: perennial setter of pole-vault records.

GAME 6

Ian is joined by two captains: Sally Gunnell, who has led Britain's women athletes; and grand slam-winning skipper Will Carling. Bill's teammates, Frank Bruno and England defender Paul Parker, provide an ideal blend of strength and composure.

☆ IAN'S TEAM ☆

SALLY GUNNELL has had to live with the nickname 'Grasshopper' at Essex Ladies, because of her speed over the hurdles. In the 1991 World Championships in Tokyo, where she captained the British women's team, Sally added a silver medal to the gold she won at the Commonwealth Games for the 400m hurdles.

WILL CARLING Who was caught last year by our Mystery Personality cameras swotting up in *Sportspages* for this encounter? Will first represented England when he was at Durham University, so he knows all about rugby union. The Harlequins centre has since become his country's youngest captain and the man who led them to the grand slams in 1991 and 1992 and the World Cup final in 1991.

☆ BILL'S TEAM ☆

FRANK BRUNO 'You know what I mean, Harry' is synonymous with the much-loved name of Franklyn Roy Bruno. He won the ABA heavyweight title back in 1980. As 'The Genie' he has become a family favourite for sparring nightly in the pantomime *Aladdin*, a part he won after playing alongside three ugly sisters, James 'Bonecrusher' Smith, Tim Witherspoon and Mike Tyson.

PAUL PARKER started his League career with Fulham. He made 153 appearances for the club between 1981 and 1987 before moving on to Queen's Park Rangers and, later, Manchester United. His international debut against Albania in 1989 paved the way for his selection for the 1990 World Cup team in which he made his presence felt most tellingly in the semi-final against West Germany, playing a part in both goals.

Pictureboard

1

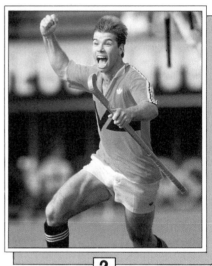

2

3

4

?

SALLY
Name the British sisters who represented different countries in the hurdles at the Commonwealth Games during the 1980s.

FRANK
Who was the first man to go the distance in a world championship title fight with Mike Tyson?

WILL
Who captained England during the 1987 World Cup in Australia?

PAUL
Which overseas player scored a hat-trick against Charlton on his League debut for Liverpool in the 1989–90 season?

IAN
Name the Australian who scored over 2000 first-class runs for Essex in the 1990 County Championship.

BILL
How did two foreign players, one a full-back and the other a lock-forward, create history when they made their debuts for Barbarians in 1990?

Pistol shooting, swimming and cross-country running are three of the five disciplines that make up the modern pentathlon. For two points, name the other two.

Tennis: Which woman player have both Sherwood Stewart and Rick Leach partnered to Wimbledon mixed doubles titles?

Soccer: Name the Scottish international who won three FA Cup winners' medals with Tottenham in the 1960s.

Athletics: English women took all three 100m hurdles medals at the 1978 Commonwealth Games. Lorna Boothe won the gold and Sharon Colyear the bronze, but who took the silver?

Rugby Union: Which man has captained his country on the most occasions?

Cricket: Who was the first man in history to take 100 catches in one-day internationals?

One-Minute Round

1 (1 pt)   Only one East German has won the 400m women's hurdles world title. Who is she?

2 (1 pt)   Motor Racing: Who was the runner-up in the world championship in both 1986 and 1987?

3 (2 pts)   Golf: On which courses did Nick Faldo win his two Open titles?

4 (1 pt)   Snooker: Name the Canadian who made a maximum in the 1988 European Open.

5 (1 pt)   Rugby Union: Who is England's most capped centre?

6 (3 pts)   Their surnames may be found at a grand prix:
a) Soccer: Ian (?)
b) Rugby: David (?)
c) Golf: Barry (?)

1 (1 pt)   Boxing: At what weight did Tom Collins fight Jeff Harding for the world title?

2 (1 pt)   Soccer: Name the last Italian club to reach successive European Cup Winners' Cup Finals.

3 (2 pts)   Kriss Akabusi, Roger Black and which other two athletes won the world championship title for the 4 × 400m in 1991?

4 (1 pt)   Bowls: Who was the last Irishman to win the World Indoor title?

5 (1 pt)   Golf: In which year did Europe and Great Britain first compete for the Ryder Cup?

6 (3 pts)   Their missing surnames are all types of music:
  a) Golf: Fred (?)
  b) Rugby Union: David (?)
  c) Horseracing: Martin (?)

GAME 6
Mystery Personality

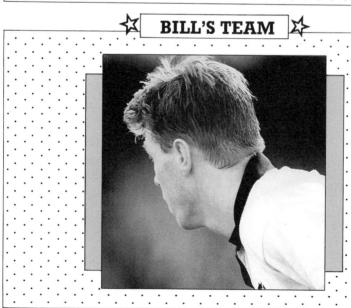

GAME 6 ANSWERS

PICTUREBOARD

1 **Evander Holyfield:** US 'heavyweight' World champion heavyweight.
2 **Steve Batchelor:** Celebrates a goal for Great Britain in the 1988 Seoul Olympics.
3 **Liz McColgan:** At the Nice Grand Prix meeting, 1987.
4 **Pita Fatialofa:** Captain of Western Samoa, Rugby World Cup, 1991.

HOME & AWAY

SALLY (HOME)
Susan and Kay Morley. Susan represented England at 400m hurdles in the 1982 Games in Brisbane, finishing fourth. Kay represented Wales and is the reigning 100m hurdles champion, winning the title in Auckland.

(AWAY)
Riding and fencing. The competition is scored on a points total for each event. It has been included in every Olympics since 1912.

FRANK (HOME)
James 'Bonecrusher' Smith. 'Bonecrusher', the first man to beat Frank, went the full 12 rounds with Tyson in Las Vegas on 7 March 1987 for both the WBC and WBA titles. Tony Tucker also went the distance in August that year before losing on points.

(AWAY)
Zina Garrison. Stewart and Garrison won the title in 1988, Garrison and Leach beat John Fitzgerald and Elizabeth Smylie in 1990.

WILL (HOME)
Mike Harrison, the Wakefield winger. Harrison (15 caps) took England to the quarter-finals, where they lost 16–3 to Wales in Brisbane.

(AWAY)
Dave Mackay. He played in the 1961 final against Leicester City, in 1962 against Burnley and in 1967 against Chelsea. He played 22 times for Scotland between 1959 and 1966.

PAUL (HOME)
Ronnie Rosenthal, the Israeli international, who joined Liverpool from Standard Liège.

(AWAY)
Shirley Strong, of Stretford AC. In Brisbane in 1982, she won the gold, with Lorna in second place. Shirley won the Olympic silver in 1984.

IAN (HOME)
Mark Waugh. He scored 2072 runs only to find himself second in the Essex averages to Graham Gooch. Mark is the brother of Test batsman Steve Waugh.

(AWAY)
Jean-Pierre Rives. Rives captained France 34 times between 1979 and 1984, winning the grand slam in 1981 and sharing the championship with Ireland in 1983. He won 59 caps during that time.

BILL (HOME)
They were the first Russians to appear in Baa-Baas colours. Igor Mironov (full-back) and Alexander Tikhonov (second row) both play for the Soviet Union and the Gagarin Academy.

(AWAY)
Allan Border. Jeffrey Dujon off Craig McDermott became his 100th catch in one-day internationals. Later in this series, Viv Richards reached his 100.

ONE-MINUTE ROUND

IAN'S TEAM
1 Sabine Busch.
2 Nigel Mansell.
3 Muirfield (1987) and St Andrews (1990).
4 Alain Robidoux.
5 Paul Dodge (32 caps).
6 a) Marshall b) Pitt c) Lane. Ian Marshall plays for Oldham Athletic. David Pitt played rugby union for Newport at centre. Barry Lane is a former winner of the Scottish Open.

BILL'S TEAM
1 Light heavyweight; he lost, in Brisbane.
2 Sampdoria: 1989, runners-up to Barcelona; 1990, winners against Anderlecht.
3 Derek Redmond and John Regis.
4 Jim Baker, in 1984.
5 1979; they lost 17–11 to the USA in West Virginia.
6 a) Funk b) Sole c) Pipe. Fred Funk plays on the US tour; David Sole is the Scottish Rugby Union captain; Martin Pipe, the National Hunt trainer, is famous for his partnership with jockey Peter Scudamore and his record 224 winners.

MYSTERY PERSONALITY

IAN'S TEAM   Gianluca Vialli: at Sampdoria's Italian League victory party, June 1991.

BILL'S TEAM   Nick Farr-Jones: Australia's Rugby World Cup captain, 1991.

GAME 7

Tonight we have the three flowers of Scotland on display. Ian has pressed his kilt and polished his bagpipes to captain Stephen Hendry and David Sole. Bill welcomes Liz McColgan, lifelong supporter of Dundee United. He hopes she will have forgiven Glenn Hysen for being in the Gothenburg team that defeated Dundee in the 1987 UEFA Cup final.

☆ BILL'S TEAM ☆

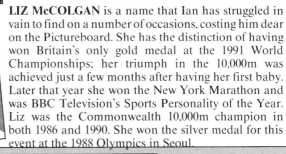

GLENN HYSEN began his career with Gothenburg with whom he won three Swedish championship titles, three Cup winners' medals and one UEFA Cup winners' medal. He eventually reached Liverpool, via PSV Eindhoven, a second term at Gothenburg and the Italian club Florentina. Glenn won a League championship medal in his first season with Liverpool in 1989, and in 1990 captained Sweden in the World Cup.

LIZ McCOLGAN is a name that Ian has struggled in vain to find on a number of occasions, costing him dear on the Pictureboard. She has the distinction of having won Britain's only gold medal at the 1991 World Championships; her triumph in the 10,000m was achieved just a few months after having her first baby. Later that year she won the New York Marathon and was BBC Television's Sports Personality of the Year. Liz was the Commonwealth 10,000m champion in both 1986 and 1990. She won the silver medal for this event at the 1988 Olympics in Seoul.

☆ IAN'S TEAM ☆

DAVID SOLE became only the third Scotsman in history to captain his country to a grand slam. Born in Aylesbury, it was while he was playing for Bath that his international career began, in 1986. He took over the Scottish captaincy from the injured Finlay Calder in 1989. The following year, in that memorable match at Murrayfield, Scotland defeated an unbeaten England to clinch the grand slam.

STEPHEN HENDRY Stephen became the youngest ever winner of the Scottish amateur championship at 15. At 16 he became the youngest player ever to join the professional ranks, and at 21 he became the youngest ever world champion. He is a Hearts supporter, loves to play golf and, unlike Ian, spends many hours watching sport on TV. With this background he should be able to answer most of Ian's questions tonight.

Pictureboard

1

2

3

4

?

GAME 7
Home & Away

GLENN
The only player to score a hat-trick during the 1988 European championships in West Germany did so against England. Who was he?

DAVID
Whose 58 caps for Ireland between 1976 and 1987 set a new world record for appearances at prop forward?

LIZ
Name the British twins who competed at the Seoul Olympics, one in the marathon, the other at 10,000m.

STEPHEN
Whose 10–8 victory over Alex Higgins in the 1990 British Open made him the first overseas player for five years to win a ranking tournament?

BILL
Who scored a try against each of the four countries in the 1986 Five Nations' championship?

IAN
Only two Englishmen have scored double Test centuries in India. Mike Gatting is one. Who is the other?

If you went up the Junction to win the Curzon Cup, what would you be doing?

Horseracing: In 1990 64,000 people turned up for the farewell appearance of a man whose career had spanned five decades in California. They were there to watch a race called the Legend's Last Ride Handicap. Who was the legend?

Swimming: Name the winner of both the 200 and 400m individual medley gold medals at the 1982 Commonwealth Games in Brisbane.

Cricket: Who in July 1990 broke Percy Fender's record for the fastest first-class century?

Swimming: Hungarian Tamas Darnyi broke two world records on his way to Olympic victories in 1988. Name either of the events.

Rugby League: Whose run of three successive victories in the Premiership final was ended by Hull in 1991?

GAME 7

One-Minute Round

1 (1 pt) Soccer: Which country ended Argentina's eight-year unbeaten run in World Cup Finals?

2 (1 pt) Tennis: Name the man who won three grand slam titles in 1988.

3 (2 pts) Swimming: Who won six gold medals at the Seoul Olympics?

4 (1 pt) Athletics: Which woman won successive world cross-country titles for England in the 1980s?

5 (1 pt) How many points are scored for a gold in archery?

6 (3 pts) These missing names are all fruits:
   a) Rugby Union: David (?)
   b) Tennis: (?) Bartkowicz
   c) Soccer: Paul (?)

1 (1 pt)   Rugby Union: Which team retained the Scottish Club Championship in 1989?

2 (1 pt)   Golf: Where did Sandy Lyle win his only Open title?

3 (2 pts)   Horseracing: On which horse did Steve Knight win the Grand National?

4 (1 pt)   Snooker: Who scored a maximum in the 1989 Scottish championship?

5 (1 pt)   Tennis: How many Wimbledon titles were won by Billie-Jean King?

6 (3 pts)   Identify these sportsmen from their nicknames:
    a) Cricket: Arkle.
    b) Boxing: The Truth.
    c) Snooker: The Grinder.

Mystery Personality

BILL'S TEAM

IAN'S TEAM

GAME 7 ANSWERS

PICTUREBOARD

1 **Zara Long:** Britain's youngest ever Olympian at 13 years old.
2 **Ryan Giggs:** Manchester United's rising star, and youngest ever Welsh international.
3 **Will Carling:** Captain of England's heroic Rugby World Cup team, 1991.
4 **Ian Baker-Finch:** Australian golfer, enjoying an apple at the 1991 US Open.

HOME & AWAY

GLENN (HOME)
Marco Van Basten of Holland. He scored five goals overall. Holland won the competition, beating the Soviet Union 2–0 in the final with goals from Van Basten and Ruud Gullit. It was the first hat-trick scored against England since 1959.

(AWAY)
Tobogganing: The start for the shortened run which opens the Cresta season. The Curzon Cup is one of two Classics of the Cresta season, the other being the Grand National.

DAVID (HOME)
Phil Orr, who played for Old Wesley. The previous record of 53 appearances was held by Graham Price of Pontypool and Wales.

(AWAY)
Willie Shoemaker, the most successful jockey of all time. During his 41-year career, from 1949 to 1990, Willie rode 8833 winners.

LIZ (HOME)
Angela and Susan Tooby. Susan finished twelfth in the marathon, Angela ran in the 10,000m but failed to qualify for the final. Angela won a Commonwealth bronze at 10,000m in 1986. Liz won the silver in Seoul at 10,000m.

(AWAY)
Lisa Curry (Australia), now Lisa Curry-Kenny. She also won the gold in the 100m butterfly, a title she won for the second time in Auckland in 1990. To add to this gold in Auckland, Lisa also won the 50m freestyle.

STEPHEN (HOME)
Bob Chaperon of Canada. In 1985 fellow Canadian Cliff Thorburn won the Goya International ranking tournament.

(AWAY)
Tom Moody, who took just 26 minutes to hit 100 for Warwickshire against Glamorgan, beating the previous record of 35 minutes, jointly held by Percy Fender and Steve O'Shaughnessy.

BILL (HOME)
Philippe Sella of France. His team shared the title with Scotland that year.

(AWAY)
200 and 400m individual medleys.

IAN (HOME)
Graeme Fowler of Lancashire. Both doubles were scored in the Fourth Test in Madras in 1985. Gatting scored 207, Fowler 201 to help England to a nine-wicket win. Fowler and Gatting put on 241 for the second wicket.

(AWAY)
Widnes. The club has won six Premiership finals and lost two.

ONE-MINUTE ROUND

BILL'S TEAM
1 Cameroon, who won 1–0 in the opening match.
2 Mats Wilander: the French, Australian and US Open championships.
3 Kristin Otto of East Germany; Matt Biondi won just five.
4 Zola Budd, in 1985 and 1986.
5 10.
6 a) Pears   b) Peaches   (c) Lemon.

IAN'S TEAM
1 Kelso.
2 Royal St George's, Sandwich, in 1985.
3 Maori Venture in 1987.
4 John Rea: He went on to win the title.
5 20 (6 singles, 10 doubles and 4 mixed).
6 a) Derek Randall   b) Carl Williams   c) Cliff Thorburn.

MYSTERY PERSONALITY

BILL'S TEAM   Jennifer Capriati: Wimbledon's youngest ever semi-finalist.

IAN'S TEAM   Jeremy Guscott: taking a breather during the Rugby World Cup in 1991.

GAME 8

Two of the nation's fastest men join the programme tonight:
Linford Christie on two legs (with Bill) and Peter Scudamore on
four (with Ian). Welshman Jonathan Davies will pick up any
rugby union points dropped by Bill's side, which is completed
by Republic of Ireland's skipper Mick McCarthy.

☆ IAN'S TEAM ☆

PETER SCUDAMORE is National Hunt racing's most successful jockey. The son of Michael Scudamore, who won the Grand National on Oxo in 1959, Peter turned professional in 1979. He has ridden more winners than any other jockey, passing John Francome's record total of 1138 in 1989. In 1989 he became the only man ever to ride more than 200 winners in a season, his total of 221 beating the previous record of 149 set by Jonjo O'Neill.

JONATHAN DAVIES Ian has not forgiven Jonathan for failing to recognise his clubmate Martin Offiah on a previous visit to the studio. Trismaran-born Jonathan attended the same South Wales school as rugby legends Carwyn James, Barry John and Gareth Davies. He made his debut for Wales in 1985 and was a key member of the side that won the triple crown in 1988. He defected to rugby league in 1989, helping Widnes to the Championship and Premiership trophies in his first season.

☆ BILL'S TEAM ☆

LINFORD CHRISTIE Born in St Andrew's, Jamaica, Linford started out as a long jumper and triple jumper. In the 1988 Seoul Olympics he became the first European to run the 100m in under ten seconds, finishing in second place. Two years later Linford won gold medals in the 100m and 4 × 100m at the Commonwealth Games and gold in the 100m at the European Championships.

MICK McCARTHY Barnsley-born Mick made his League debut at Oakwell in 1977. His route to Millwall FC has been via Manchester City, which he helped to win promotion to the First Division; Celtic, with whom he won League Championship and Cup Winners' Cup medals; and French League club Lyon. He was in the Republic of Ireland team that reached the European Championship Finals in 1988 and skippered them in the World Cup Finals in Italy in 1990.

GAME 8
Pictureboard

1

2

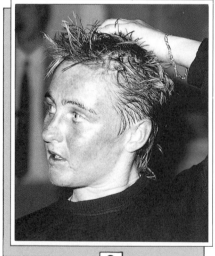

3

4

?

GAME 8
Home & Away

PETER
Which jockey parted company with Rinus in the 1991 Grand National, so ending a remarkable run of seven finishes in seven Nationals?

Swimming: Anthony Nesty gave which country its first Olympic gold medal in 1988?

LINFORD
Which athlete achieved the 100 and 200m double at successive Commonwealth Games during the 1970s?

It's played over four periods of 15 minutes. Only two of the seven players on each side can score. Australia have been outright world champions four times and New Zealand twice. What's the sport?

JONATHAN
Which player holds the record for the most tries scored in a career in Challenge Cup finals at Wembley?

The Jack Murphy Stadium hosted which national event in January 1988?

MICK
Name the Irishman who has scored both for and against Manchester United in FA Cup finals.

Motor Racing: Name the driver who clocked up his 200th grand prix at Silverstone in 1990.

IAN
The openers for which county both scored over 2000 first-class runs in the 1990 championship season?

Golf: Turnberry is a 577-yard par five and is the longest hole on an Open championship course. The Postage Stamp is a 126-yard par three, and is the shortest. They are both found on the front nine of which course?

BILL
Who in 1988 won an international cap for England despite being on the field of play for only three seconds?

The Brasenose Four won a major race but were disqualified for dropping a member of their team. They then changed the rules of their sport to create a new event. What new event did they create?

GAME 8

One-Minute Round

1 (1 pt) Rugby League: Who in 1989 became the youngest player to win a Great Britain cap?

2 (1 pt) Motor Racing: How many grand prix races did Jackie Stewart win?

3 (2 pts) Tennis: Chris Evert lost four Wimbledon Ladies' singles finals in the 1980s. A point for each of the winners.

4 (1 pt) Horseracing: Which of David Elsworth's horses won the 1990 Irish Grand National?

5 (1 pt) American Football: For which team does John Elway play quarterback?

6 (3 pts) The following missing names are all found on the golf course:
   a) Boxing: (?) Jay
   b) Soccer: Alan (?)
   c) Golf: Ken (?)

BILL'S TEAM

1 (1 pt)   Soccer: Which player-manager scored a First Division hat-trick against Aston Villa in 1990?

2 (1 pt)   Golf: How many major tournaments has Jack Nicklaus won?

3 (2 pts)   Cricket: Somerset are the only county to have successfully defended the Benson and Hedges Cup. Which teams did they beat in the two finals?

4 (1 pt)   Name the European city that staged the Olympic Games prior to Barcelona in 1992.

5 (1 pt)   Athletics: In which event did Eamonn Coghlan win a gold medal at the World Championships in 1983?

6 (3 pts)   The missing names are all parts of a car:
    a) Cricket: Percy (?)
    b) Rugby Union: Geoff (?)
    c) Boxing: Darrin Van (?)

GAME 8
Mystery Personality

☆ **BILL'S TEAM** ☆

GAME 8 ANSWERS

PICTUREBOARD

1 **Ayrton Senna:** Facing the press, Belgium, 1991.
2 **Seppo Raty:** Setting a new World Record, Finland, June 1991.
3 **Lisa Opie:** 1991 British Open Squash Champion, from Guernsey in the Channel Islands.
4 **Brian Moore:** England rugby star, practising for the line-out.

HOME & AWAY

PETER (HOME)
Neil Doughty. Rinus fell on the second circuit. In 1990 Neil was third on Rinus. He won the race in 1984 on Hallo Dandy.

(AWAY)
Surinam, in the 100m butterfly.

LINFORD (HOME)
Don Quarrie of Jamaica, in both 1970 and 1974.

(AWAY)
Netball. Only the goal-attack and the goal shooter can score.

JONATHAN (HOME)
Kevin Iro of Wigan, with six. He scored two tries in Wigan's 36–14 win against Warrington at Wembley. He also scored two tries in the 1989 final against St Helens, and two tries in the 1988 final against Halifax.

(AWAY)
Superbowl XXII. The Jack Murphy Stadium is the home of the San Diego Chargers (American football) and the San Diego Padres (baseball team).

MICK (HOME)
Frank Stapleton. Stapleton scored for Arsenal in their 3–2 win over Manchester United in 1979. He scored for United in the 1983 final against Brighton which ended 2–2, with United winning the replay 4–0.

(AWAY)
Ricardo Patrese of Italy. His first grand prix was in 1977 at Monaco.

IAN (HOME)
Glamorgan. The batsmen were Alan Butcher and Hugh Morris. Butcher scored six centuries in his tally of 2116 runs. Ten centuries were among Morris's 2276 total.

(AWAY)
Troon. Turnberry is the sixth. The Postage Stamp is the eighth. The Open has been staged there six times.

BILL (HOME)
Dave Egerton of Bath. He came on as a replacement for the injured Gary Rees in England's 25 points to 12 victory over Fiji in Suva.

(AWAY)
The Coxless Fours. The Four ordered their cox out of the boat before the start of the Stewards Cup at Henley in 1868. One man lighter, they won the race but were disqualified. The following year there was a race for coxless fours.

ONE-MINUTE ROUND

IAN'S TEAM
1 Paul Newlove of Featherstone. He was 18 years and 72 days old and beat the record set by Shaun Edwards, who was capped aged 18 years and 135 days against France in 1985.
2 27.
3 Evonne Cawley, in 1980; Martina Navratilova, in 1982, 1984 and 1985.
4 Desert Orchid.
5 Denver Broncos.
6 a) Tee b) Rough c) Green.

BILL'S TEAM
1 Trevor Francis, for QPR v Aston Villa.
2 18.
3 Surrey, in 1981; Nottinghamshire, in 1982.
4 Moscow, in 1980.
5 5000m.
6 a) Fender b) Wheel c) Horn.

MYSTERY PERSONALITY

IAN'S TEAM   Karen Straker: all dressed up for the Seoul Olympics.

BILL'S TEAM   Leroy Burrell: US sprinter in serious mood in Monte Carlo in 1991.

GAME 9

Three South Londoners and a Kiwi join our captains tonight.
Steve Davis and Wayne Shelford team up with Ian to do battle
with Bill's line-up of Zara Long and Tony Cascarino.

☆ BILL'S TEAM ☆

TONY CASCARINO This Englishman with an Italian name played football in Scotland with Celtic and is a Republic of Ireland cap. He has now eased his international relations by signing for Chelsea in London. Despite the large fees he now commands, Tony has not forgotten that he was bought from the Kentish team Crocken Hill by Gillingham for twelve tracksuits, two footballs and six sheets of corrugated iron. Tony was a member of the Republic side that did so well in the 1988 European Championships, and played in all of Ireland's games in the 1990 World Cup Finals.

ZARA LONG is so often identifiable only by her white cap with a Union Jack emblazoned on the side as she fights through the white-water fury created by eight lanes of competitive swimmers. She made her Olympic debut aged 13 in Los Angeles, and just two years later won two silver medals at the Commonwealth Games.

☆ IAN'S TEAM ☆

STEVE DAVIS MBE turned professional in 1978 and dominated snooker during the 1980s, winning the World and United Kingdom titles six times each. His victory in the 1989 Rothman's Grand Prix was his 50th major professional title. He waited two years until January 1992 for his next world ranking title, the Mercantile Credit classic, defeating Stephen Hendry 9–8. On the *Question of Sport* stage, Steve 'interesting' Davis, as he refers to himself, has a sharp dry humour which more than makes up for his lack of sporting knowledge.

WAYNE SHELFORD The North Harbour and now Northampton number 8 made his debut for the All Blacks in 1986. A year later he took over the captaincy, leading them to 14 consecutive victories in internationals. For those who think he will be under pressure tonight because he has not seen the programme before – forget it. Wayne has appeared as a guest on the New Zealand version of the show on three occasions.

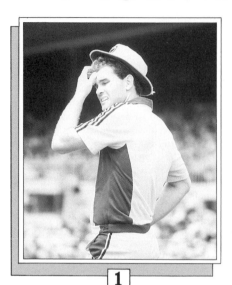

1

2

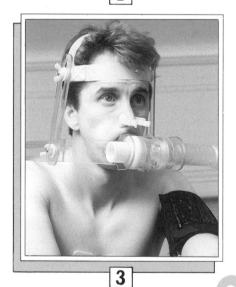

3

4

?

GAME 9
Home & Away

TONY
Two players scored their first goals for England during the 1990 World Cup in Italy. David Platt was one. Who was the other?

STEVE
Who in the 1990 World Championship became the first player to make a 16-red total clearance?

ZARA
Which woman swimmer won a record five gold medals at the 1990 Commonwealth Games in Auckland?

WAYNE
The prop who has captained New Zealand on most occasions did so between 1958 and 1965. Who was he?

BILL
The world record for an international second row partnership is 27 games. It is currently held by Alan Martin and which other player?

IAN
Who in 1990 became the first Surrey batsman for 19 years to score 2000 first class runs in a season?

In which sport could a clutch shooter 'cherrypick' to defeat a Diamond and One?

The only winner of the Cesarewitch, the St Leger, and the Derby twice is?

Who in 1979 became the first British girl to break two minutes for the 800m?

In which sport is it an advantage to get into the 'Egg position'?

Who was the only Briton to finish in the first three in a 500cc grand prix during the 1990 season?

Name the last horse to carry twelve stones to victory in the Grand National.

One-Minute Round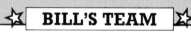

☆ **BILL'S TEAM** ☆

1 (1 pt) Soccer: Who is the most capped Republic of Ireland international?

2 (1 pt) Darts: Who did Bob Anderson defeat in the 1988 World Championship final?

3 (2 pts) Swimming: At which events did Sarah Hardcastle win Gold medals at the 1986 Commonwealth Games?

4 (1 pt) Golf: Name the last Briton to win the US Open.

5 (1 pt) Motor racing: What colour is the warning flag?

6 (3 pts) Name the winners of the following events in 1987:
a) Soccer: FA Cup.
b) Cricket: County Championship.
c) American Football: Superbowl.

1 (1 pt)   Rugby Union: Who is New Zealand's most capped number 8?

2 (1 pt)   Snooker: Which player did Ray Reardon beat twice in world finals?

3 (2 pts)   Tennis: Hana Mandlikova lost two Wimbledon finals in the 1980s. Who were the champions?

4 (1 pt)   Boxing: Name the Canadian who won the world light heavyweight title in the 1980s.

5 (1 pt)   Soccer: What are Plymouth Argyle's home colours?

6 (3 pts)   Name the world champions of these events in 1985:
a) Snooker: ?
b) Women's squash: ?
c) Motor racing: ?

GAME 9
Mystery Personality

GAME 9 ANSWERS

PICTUREBOARD

1 **Martin Crowe:** New Zealand's cricket captain.
2 **Norbert Rozsa:** Hungarian swimmer, setting a new 100m breaststroke World Record.
3 **Greg LeMond:** The US's premier Tour de France expert.
4 **Michael Lynagh:** Star of Australia's Rugby World Cup team, 1991.

HOME & AWAY

TONY (HOME)
Mark Wright of Derby County. He scored the winner against Egypt, Platt's goal was against Belgium. Platt also scored against Cameroon and Italy.

(AWAY)
Basketball. A clutch shooter is the name given to a player who is relied upon to score vital baskets. A cherrypicker is an attacking player who remains in close proximity to the basket, and a Diamond and One is a defensive strategy.

STEVE (HOME)
Steve James. He achieved this feat in his first-round match against Alex Higgins, which he won 10–5. James was helped by a free ball, which meant he could count a colour as an extra red. His break was 135. It was the first 16-red total clearance in a ranking tournament.

(AWAY)
Mick the Miller. He won the Derby in 1929 and 1930, the Cesarewitch in 1930, and the St Leger in 1931. He won on 46 of his 61 outings, which included a run of 19 successive victories.

ZARA (HOME)
Hayley Lewis of Australia. She won the 200 and 400m freestyle, the 200m butterfly, the 400m individual medley, as well as a gold in the 4 × 200m freestyle. She also won a bronze in the 200m individual medley.

(AWAY)
Christina Boxer (Cahill), in Torino on 4 August 1979 with a time of 1.59.05. This has since been beaten by Kirsty McDermott (1985) with a time of 1.57.42.

WAYNE (HOME)
Wilson Whineray of Canterbury, Waikato and Auckland. He captained the All Blacks on 30 occasions and had 32 caps to his credit.

(AWAY)
Skiing. It's a position which provides minimum wind resistance.

BILL (HOME)
Geoff Wheel, for Wales between 1974 and 1981. Martin won 34 caps, and Wheel 32.

(AWAY)
Niall McKenzie. With two third places to his credit, Niall finished fourth in the world championship rankings on his Suzuki. Wayne Rainey took the world title.

IAN (HOME)
David Ward. He scored 2072 runs, including seven centuries, at an average of 76.74. In 1971 John Edrich scored 2031 runs at an average of 47.23.

(AWAY)
Red Rum, in the 1974 Grand National, his second win in the race.

ONE-MINUTE ROUND

BILL'S TEAM
1 Liam Brady, with 72 caps.
2 John Lowe.
3 400 and 800m freestyle.
4 Tony Jacklin, in 1970.
5 Yellow.
6 a) Coventry City   b) Nottinghamshire   c) New York Giants.

IAN'S TEAM
1 Murray Mexted, with 34 caps 1979–85.
2 Eddie Charlton, in 1973 and 1975.
3 Chris Evert, in 1981; and Martina Navratilova, in 1986.
4 Donny Lalonde.
5 Green.
6 a) Dennis Taylor   b) Susan Devoy   c) Alain Prost.

MYSTERY PERSONALITY

BILL'S TEAM   Serge Blanco: legendary French rugby player.

IAN'S TEAM   Michael Thomas: star of Liverpool's midfield.

GAME 10

This special game gives us an opportunity to look back over the decade with the help of all the captains who have led the teams during that period.

☆ IAN'S TEAM ☆

EMLYN HUGHES 'Crazy Horse' began his football League career with Blackpool before moving to Liverpool in 1967. With the Merseysiders Emlyn won four championship medals, an FA Cup medal, two UEFA Cups and two European Cup Winners' medals. He moved to Wolves in 1979 where he won the one major honour that had eluded him at Liverpool – a League Cup winners medal. Emlyn was a captain of *A Question of Sport* on 122 occasions between 1979 and 1988.

GARETH EDWARDS faced teams led by Emlyn Hughes on *A Question of Sport* 36 times between 1979 and 1981. The Cardiff, Wales and British Lions scrum half played for his country a record 53 times in succession between 1967 and 1978. His tally of 20 tries at scrum-half is also an international record. During the Edwards era Wales won seven International Championships, five Triple Crowns and two grand slams. He went on three Lions tours in 1968, 1971, and 1974.

☆ BILL'S TEAM ☆

WILLIE CARSON Willie has ridden over 2000 winners in a career spanning five decades. His record on *A Question of Sport* is only slightly less impressive: captaining opposite Bill on 26 occasions during 1981 and 1982. In 1988 he made British turf history by becoming the first man to ride a Classic winner that he had bred himself; Minster Son in the St Leger. April 1990 saw him complete the set of English Classics by winning the 1000 Guineas on Salsabil.

BRENDAN FOSTER was captain for eight programmes in 1977, in opposition to Henry Cooper. The high spots in Brendan's ten-year international athletics career included two world records: in 1973 he bettered Lasse Viren's time over two miles and the following year Emile Puttemans' over 3000m. He won a European Championship gold medal in 1974 at 5000m and a Commonwealth Games gold at 10,000m in 1978.

GAME 10
Pictureboard

1

2

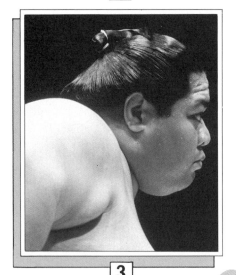

3

4

?

GAME 10
Home & Away

EMLYN
Which player scored in a European final, an FA Cup final and a League Cup final during the 1980s?

Bridgehampton, Sebring. and Riverside are all famous what?

WILLIE
Name the last Derby winner to sire a Derby winner.

In which sport did Robert Fulford, a 21-year-old Durham University student, win the world title and a prize of £25 by defeating Blackburn's Mark Saurin in London in 1990?

GARETH
Which team has appeared in a record nine Welsh Cup finals?

Athletics: Which 16-year-old became Britain's youngest ever Olympic medallist when the 4×400m relay team won bronze in 1980?

BRENDAN
Who won the 1978 Commonwealth 1500m and four years later broke the world record for the 5000m?

Cricket: Name the Australian who scored a century on his Test debut during the 1990–91 series against England.

IAN
In 1897 Archie McLaren became the first English player in history to score a century in his first Test match as captain. Which England captain equalled McLaren's achievement 93 years later?

Which British athlete shares his christian name with a character from Shakespeare's play *The Tempest*?

BILL
Who in November 1990 equalled Mike Gibson's world record of 81 international appearances?

Soccer: Scotland's only victory in the 1990 World Cup Finals was against which country?

GAME 10
One-Minute Round

1 (1 pt)   Soccer: Which Second Division team defeated Arsenal 1–0 in the 1980 FA Cup final?

2 (1 pt)   Golf: Name the only European player to win the Open in the 1970s.

3 (2 pts) Cricket: Two players made their 100th Test match appearance in the 1989 Pakistan v India series. Who were they?

4 (1 pt)   Rugby Union: who was the last Welshman to captain the British Lions?

5 (1 pt)   Horseracing: Which jockey rode Mr Frisk to victory in the 1990 Grand National?

6 (3 pts) Which pantomimes have featured the following?
   a) Frank Bruno as the Genie.
   b) Barry McGuigan as the Henchman.
   c) Liz Hobbs as the Princess.

1 (1 pt)   Horseracing: Which jockey won three English Classics in 1985?

2 (1 pt)   Tennis: With whom did John McEnroe win four Wimbledon men's doubles titles?

3 (2 pts)   Golf: Which two golfers won the Open at Muirfield in the 1980s?

4 (1 pt)   Athletics: Name the 1980 Olympic champion at 5000 and 10,000m.

5 (1 pt)   Motor racing: Who was the last American to win the World Formula One title?

6 (3 pts)   Which pantomimes have featured the following?
   a) Ian Botham as the king.
   b) Geoff Capes as the captain.
   c) Tessa Sanderson as Girl Friday.

GAME 10
Mystery Personality

☆ IAN'S TEAM ☆

☆ BILL'S TEAM ☆

GAME 10 ANSWERS

PICTUREBOARD

1 **Jose Maria Olazabal:** Getting a round in, French Open, 1991.
2 **Graham Bell:** One of Great Britain's leading skiers and younger brother of Martin.
3 **Konishiki** (the Dump Truck): Japan's most famous Sumo export.
4 **Clive Rice:** Nottinghamshire and South Africa cricketer.

HOME & AWAY

EMLYN (HOME)
Andy Gray. He scored for Everton in the 1985 European Cup Winners' Cup final against Rapid Vienna; and, again for Everton, in the 1984 FA Cup Final; and in the 1980 League Cup final for Wolves against Nottingham Forest, his winning goal allowing Emlyn to lift the one domestic prize that had always eluded him. Emlyn got the answer wrong on the show.

(AWAY)
American motor racing circuits. Bridgehampton is a four-mile sportscar circuit. Sebring is a venue for the World Sportscar Championship and was the venue for the 1959 US Formula One Grand Prix, as was Riverside in 1960.

WILLIE (HOME)
Shirley Heights. He won the Derby in 1978, ridden by Greville Starkey, and then sired the 1985 winner Slip Anchor, ridden by Steve Cauthen.

(AWAY)
Croquet, in the final at the Hurlingham Club. He failed to retain the title in 1991.

GARETH (HOME)
Llanelli. The club has won seven of its nine finals, in 1973, 1974, 1975, 1976, 1985, 1988 and 1991. Its two defeats were in 1972 and 1989.

(AWAY)
Lindsey MacDonald. She was aged 16 years and 171 days. The other team members were Michelle Probert, Joslyn Hoyte-Smith and Janine MacGregor.

BRENDAN (HOME)
David Moorcroft. He won the Commonwealth 1500m title in Edmonton in 3 min 35.48 sec. In Oslo in July 1982 he clocked a time of 13 min 00.41 sec to set a new world record in the 5000m.

(AWAY)
Mark Waugh. He scored his century (138) in the Fourth Test in Adelaide, which ended in a draw.

IAN (HOME)
Allan Lamb. He captained England for the first time in the Fourth Test against the West Indies in Barbados in 1990, and scored 119 runs. Lamb assumed the captaincy after Graham Gooch broke his hand in the Third Test. McLaren scored 109 in the First Test against Australia in Sydney.

(AWAY)
Sebastian Coe.

BILL (HOME)
Serge Blanco of France. He equalled the eleven-year-old record in the Second Test against New Zealand.

(AWAY)
Sweden, the only European country to lose all their games in Italy. Interestingly, they had topped England's qualifying group.

ONE-MINUTE ROUND

IAN'S TEAM
1 West Ham United.
2 Severiano Ballesteros, in 1979 at Lytham.
3 Kapil Dev (India), in the First Test in Karachi; and Javed Miandad (Pakistan) in the Second Test in Faislabad. Miandad became the sixth highest Test run-maker in the process.
4 Phil Bennett, on the 1977 tour to New Zealand and Fiji.
5 Marcus Armytage. Mr Frisk won in the record time of 8 min 47.8 sec.
6 a) Aladdin   b) Snow White   c) Jack and the Beanstalk.

BILL'S TEAM
1 Steve Cauthen. He partnered the filly Oh So Sharp to victories in the 1000 Guineas and the St Leger, and Slip Anchor in the Derby.
2 Peter Fleming.
3 Tom Watson, in 1980; and Nick Faldo, in 1987.
4 Miruts Yifter of Ethiopia.
5 Mario Andretti, in 1978.
6 a) Jack and the Beanstalk   b) Dick Whittington   c) Robinson Crusoe.

MYSTERY PERSONALITY

IAN'S TEAM   Graeme Hick: England batsman, at home in Zimbabwe.

BILL'S TEAM   Brian Moore: Harlequins and England. Can't face it any more.

GAME 11

If high scoring is required, or just keeping the opposition at bay, both captains have the right guests in this game. Bill lines up with Eric Bristow and Gary Lineker. Ian is joined by the England fly-half Rob Andrew and long-jumper Fiona May.

⭐ BILL'S TEAM ⭐

ERIC BRISTOW The 'Crafty Cockney' expects to average over 90 with every trip to the ocky. Eric dominated the Embassy world darts championships during the 1980s, winning it on five occasions. His first world title came in 1980, when he was just 22 years old. Born in London's East End, Eric has now settled in the Midlands which he says 'is the centre of the country and you can be anywhere in two-and-a-half hours'.

GARY LINEKER is a prolific goal scorer, with almost 200 League goals to his credit. His goals in the Mexico World Cup signalled that he was ready for the 'big time'. Barcelona, managed by Terry Venables, paid £2.75 million for his services. Gary won his first major honour with Barcelona, a European Cup Winners' Cup medal. He came back to Britain in 1989 to join Terry at White Hart Lane. In 1991 Spurs won the FA cup, beating Nottingham Forest 2–1, giving Gary his second major honour.

⭐ IAN'S TEAM ⭐

ROB ANDREW won Blues at Cambridge University in both rugby and cricket. The Wasps, England and British Lions fly-half is used to making a large contribution to his team's score – thankfully for Ian, who needs all the points he can get. In 1986 Rob scored all 21 of England's points against Wales at Twickenham. As a former Yorkshire second-team player Rob will also be able to help Ian with his cricket questions.

FIONA MAY started her athletics career as a sprinter and high jumper before taking up long-jumping at the age of thirteen. As a nineteen-year-old she won the World Student Games long-jump title in Canada in 1988 with a leap of 6.82m. To put her performance into perspective: that jump was six centimetres better than the world record set by Britain's gold medal winner Mary Bignal Rand at the 1964 Olympics.

1

2

3

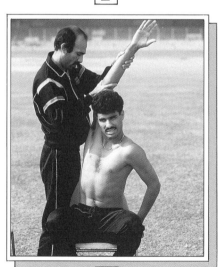

4

?

GAME 11
Home & Away

ERIC
The former world champion and world number one Bob Anderson was knocked out of the 1990 Embassy World Championship by which overseas player?

ROB
Which player has been the fastest to reach 100, 200, 300 and 400 points in an international rugby career?

GARY
Which Newcastle striker was the League's leading goalscorer in all competitions in the 1989–90 season?

FIONA
Name the last British woman long jumper to win an Olympic medal.

BILL
Which Oxford graduate led the All Blacks to victory in the 1987 World Cup?

IAN
Name the Warwickshire bowler who took 78 first class wickets in 1990, 16 less than the leading wicket taker Neil Foster.

Boxing: Name the only man to have held both world cruiserweight and world heavyweight titles.

Horseracing: Which horse won Cheltenham Gold Cups in successive years in the 1970s?

Athletics: At which event has Senegal's El Hadji Amadou dia Ba won an Olympic medal?

In which sport do you compete for the Hattersley Salver?

Cricket: Which team won most county championships in the 1970s?

Rugby League: Who captained Australia to victory in the 1989 World Cup?

One-Minute Round

 ☆ **BILL'S TEAM** ☆

1 (1 pt) Darts: Who won three successive World Masters titles in the 1980s?

2 (1 pt) Soccer: Which Second Division club reached the final of the League Cup in 1990?

3 (2 pts) Horseracing: Sadeem was ridden to successive Ascot Gold Cup victories by different jockeys. Name them.

4 (1 pt) Golf: Who was the first player to win five World Matchplay titles?

5 (1 pt) Horseracing: Which is the most northerly British race course?

6 (3 pts) The missing surnames are all pop groups:
   a) Fencing: Mark (?)
   b) Golf: Jodie (?)
   c) Soccer: Gerry (?)

1 (1 pt)   Rugby Union: Name the man who made his international debut at fly-half for Ireland in 1990 having previously played for Australia.

2 (1 pt)   At which sport was Karen Briggs four times world champion in the 1980s?

3 (2 pts)   Motor Racing: Two South Americans have won the British Grand Prix in the 1970s. Name them.

4 (1 pt)   Athletics: Who is the reigning Commonwealth Games women's long jump champion?

5 (1 pt)   Tennis: Who did Boris Becker defeat in his first Wimbledon men's singles final?

6 (3 pts)   The following missing surnames are all things you can do with hair:
     a) Soccer: Keith (?)
     b) Cricket: John (?)
     c) Rugby League: Andy.(?)

GAME 11
Mystery Personality

GAME 11 ANSWERS

PICTUREBOARD

1 **Paula Thomas and Simone Jacobs:** Members of Britain's sprint relay squad.
2 **David Wheaton:** US tennis star, in agony v Boris Becker at Wimbledon, 1991.
3 **Phil Taylor:** World Darts Champion in 1990 and 1992.
4 **Waqar Younis:** Surrey and Pakistan pace bowler.

HOME & AWAY

ERIC (HOME)
Jan Hoffman of Denmark, who beat Anderson, the 1988 world champion, 3–2. Hoffman took up darts after watching the sport on BBC Television.

(AWAY)
Evander Holyfield. The US boxer became world cruiserweight champion in 1986, and held both the WBA and IBF versions.

ROB (HOME)
Grant Fox of New Zealand. He reached 100 points in his sixth match, 200 in his thirteenth match, 300 in his eighteenth match, and scored his 400th point against France in November 1990, his 25th international.

(AWAY)
L'Escargot. He won in 1970 and 1971, ridden by Tommy Carberry and trained by D. Moore. Only three horses have ever won more than two Gold Cups: Arkle, Golden Miller and Cottage Rake. L'Escargot won the Grand National in 1975, again with Tommy Carberry in the saddle.

GARY (HOME)
Mick Quinn of Newcastle. He scored 36 goals, 32 of them in Second Division games.

(AWAY)
400m hurdles. He won the silver in 1988, splitting the Americans Andre Phillips and Ed Moses.

FIONA (HOME)
Sue Hearnshaw. She won the bronze medal in Los Angeles in 1984, with a leap of 6m 80cm. Two Romanians took the major honours: Anisoara Stanciu (gold) and Vali Ionescu (silver).

(AWAY)
Lacrosse. The trophy is competed for by women only.

BILL (HOME)
David Kirk. Scrum-half Kirk took over the captaincy when Andy Dalton was injured. He played so well that Dalton was unable to regain his place.

IAN (HOME)
Tim Munton. Foster (Essex) took 94 wickets.

(AWAY)
Kent, with three championships, in 1970, 1977 (shared with Middlesex) and 1978.

(AWAY)
Wally Lewis. Australia beat New Zealand in the final.

ONE-MINUTE ROUND

BILL'S TEAM
1 Bob Anderson, in 1986, 1987 and 1988.
2 Oldham Athletic, losing 1–0 to Notts Forest.
3 Greville Starkey, in 1988; and Willie Carson in 1989.
4 Gary Player, in 1965, 1966, 1968, 1971 and 1973.
5 Perth.
6 a) Slade   b) Mudd   c) Queen.

IAN'S TEAM
1 Brian Smith.
2 Judo; extra-lightweight in 1982, 1984, 1986 and 1989.
3 Emerson Fittipaldi, in 1972 and 1975; and Carlos Reutemann in 1978.
4 Jane Flemming of Australia.
5 Kevin Curren, in 1985.
6 a) Curle   b) Dye   c) Platt.

MYSTERY PERSONALITY

BILL'S TEAM   Richie Richardson: flamboyant West Indies batsman and captain.

IAN'S TEAM   Duke McKenzie: the UK's popular WBO World bantamweight champion, plus referee.

GAME 12

Ian is joined by Laura Davies and Chris Eubank. Bill lines up with athlete Steve Backley and footballer Dean Saunders.

☆ IAN'S TEAM ☆

LAURA DAVIES started playing golf at the age of thirteen just to keep her brother company. She became the leading money earner on the ladies' European Tour in her first season as a professional, in 1984. Two years later she repeated this feat and also added the British Open title to her collection of wins. As if to prove that this was no fluke, Laura won the US Open ladies' title, beating the United States contingent in their own backyard and notching up a first for British women golfers.

CHRIS EUBANK 5 November 1990, the night that he took the world middleweight title, was memorable on several counts. After the hard-fought contest, Chris surprised the millions watching on television by proposing to his beloved Sharon. That emotional moment has tended to obscure the magnitude of his achievement. Fight fans, however, will know that he is only the fifth British boxer this century to win the world middleweight crown.

☆ BILL'S TEAM ☆

STEVE BACKLEY became the first British man to break the world javelin record, with a throw of 89.58m in Stockholm on 2 July 1991. Three weeks later at Crystal Palace he was at it again – his throw of 90.88m was the first world record set by a Briton in Britain since Dave Bedford's historic 10,000m triumph seventeen years earlier.

DEAN SAUNDERS The Liverpool and Wales striker began his professional career with Swansea City. He did a spell at Oxford before moving to Brighton and then, in 1985, to the Baseball ground at Derby. He was one of the First Division's elite, with a £1m price tag. Dean's exciting partnership with Ian Rush at international level brought him to the attention of Liverpool. When Derby County suffered a cash shortage in the summer of 1991 they bid £2.5 million to bring him to Merseyside.

GAME 12
Pictureboard

1

2

3

4

?

Home & Away

LAURA
Liselotte Neumann won the US Open in 1988, making her the first golfer, male or female, to win a major title for which country?

STEVE
Name the Hungarian family that won gold medals at both the 1948 and 1976 Olympic Games.

CHRIS
Which British boxer contested three world title fights in the 1980s, losing on each occasion? Two of the contests were at middleweight and the third was at light heavyweight.

DEAN
Which player came on as a substitute in the 1990 FA Cup final and scored two goals?

IAN
Which English bowler took a record thirteen wickets in a Test match in the West Indies?

BILL
Who captained England on their 1984 tour of South Africa?

Athletics: Name the Briton who won the 1986 European 5000m title.

If you have just fallen from a Dumper into the Soup, where are you?

Hockey: Which country won the women's Olympic gold medal at the 1980 Games in Moscow?

Squash: The semi-finals of the 1990 British Open were reached by which Australian brother and sister?

Swimming: Whose five-year-old 100m breaststroke world record was broken by Adrian Moorhouse in 1989?

Eventing: On which horse did Mark Todd successfully defend his individual Olympic title?

GAME 12
One-Minute Round

1 (1 pt)   Athletics: The winner of the men's gold medal for the javelin at the 1987 World Championships was?

2 (1 pt)   In which sport was John Price a world champion?

3 (2 pts)   Golf: The American Larry Mize won the US Masters title in 1987 after a three-way play off. A point for each of the other two golfers.

4 (1 pt)   Soccer: Who scored Scotland's only goal in the 1986 World Cup Finals?

5 (1 pt)   Tennis: Which nation reached the Davis Cup final seven times during the 1980s?

6 (3 pts)   Name the winners of these events in 1983:
   a) World Darts.
   b) Rugby League Challenge Cup.
   c) Badminton Horse Trials.

1 (1 pt)   Golf: Who won the British Women's Open Championship twice in the 1980s?

2 (1 pt)   Snooker: Who was the only Welshman to win the United Kingdom title twice?

3 (2 pts)   Boxing: Two Britons challenged Mike McCallum for the world middleweight title. Name them.

4 (1 pt)   Athletics: Who was the only British woman to win a gold medal at the 1990 European Championships?

5 (1 pt)   Golf: On which course did Mark Calcavecchia win the Open title?

6 (3 pts)   Name the beaten finalists of these events in 1986:
     a) Snooker: World Championship.
     b) Golf: World Matchplay.
     c) Tennis: Ladies' singles at Wimbledon.

GAME 12
Mystery Personality

☆ IAN'S TEAM ☆

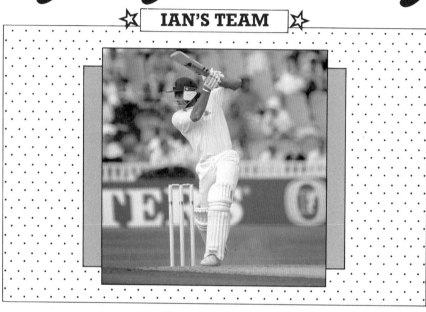

☆ BILL'S TEAM ☆

GAME 12 ANSWERS

PICTUREBOARD

1 **Bernhard Langer:** Celebrating a putt in the 1987 Ryder Cup.
2 **John Elway:** Quarterback for the Denver Broncos.
3 **Dan O'Brien:** US decathlete, star of the future.
4 **Alberto Tomba:** Italian skiing superstar and first man ever to retain the Olympic Giant Slalom title, at Albertville in 1992.

HOME & AWAY

LAURA (HOME)
Switzerland. She became the third European woman to win the US Open. Laura became the second in 1987.

(AWAY)
Jack Buckner. He took the gold in a time of 13.10.15. Tim Hutchings was third.

STEVE (HOME)
Imre and Miklos Nemeth. Miklos won the gold for the javelin in Montreal in 1976. His father, Imre, won the gold for the hammer in London. They are the only father and son to win Olympic golds.

(AWAY)
In the sea. A Dumper is one of those rogue waves on which it is impossible to surf. The Soup is the white water which follows the crashing of a wave.

CHRIS (HOME)
Tony Sibson. Sibson's two losses at middleweight were to Marvin Hagler in February 1983, in the sixth round; and to Frank Tate in February 1988. At light heavyweight he lost to Britain's Dennis Andries, in the ninth round, in September 1986.

(AWAY)
Zimbabwe. They were the only unbeaten side in the tournament. Czechoslovakia took silver and the Soviet Union the bronze.

DEAN (HOME)
Ian Wright of Crystal Palace. Wright had missed most of the season through injury. Palace lost the final after a replay to Manchester United.

(AWAY)
Rodney and Michelle Martin. Rodney lost to Jahangir Khan in the final, Jahangir's record ninth title. His sister Michelle was beaten by Susan Devoy in the semi-final. The other brother, Brett, reached the semi-final of the European Open in 1990.

IAN (HOME)
Tony Greig. He took 8 for 86 in the first innings and 5 for 70 in the second innings of the Fifth Test in Port of Spain, Trinidad, in 1974.

(AWAY)
Steve Lundquist. His time of 1 min 01.65 sec was set in the Olympic final of 1984 in Los Angeles. Moorhouse's record was also beaten by Norbert Rozsa of Hungary.

BILL (HOME)
John Scott of Cardiff. Bill captained the last Lions tour to South Africa in 1980.

(AWAY)
Charisma. Todd won in 1984 in Los Angeles, and retained the title in Seoul in 1988.

ONE-MINUTE ROUND

IAN'S TEAM
1 Seppo Raty of Finland.
2 Indoor Bowls (Wales).
3 Seve Ballesteros and Greg Norman.
4 Gordon Strachan, in the game with West Germany. Scotland lost 2–1.
5 Sweden.
6 a) Keith Deller   b) Featherstone Rovers   c) Lucinda Green.

BILL'S TEAM
1 Debbie Massey of the USA, in 1980 and 1981.
2 Doug Mountjoy, in 1978 and 1988.
3 Herol Graham and Michael Watson.
4 Yvonne Murray, in the 3000m.
5 Royal Troon.
6 a) Steve Davis   b) Sandy Lyle   c) Hana Mandlikova.

MYSTERY PERSONALITY

IAN'S TEAM   Mark Ramprakash: Middlesex and England star.

BILL'S TEAM   Marc Girardelli: concentrating before a run at Val D'Isere.

GAME 13

Figureskater Joanne Conway and the Everton and Scotland midfielder Stuart McCall join Bill, while athlete Peter Elliott and showjumper Nick Skelton team up with Ian Botham.

☆ BILL'S TEAM ☆

JOANNE CONWAY Since Jeanette Altwegg won the world title back in 1951 no British woman has won a world individual figure skating title. John Curry showed the way for the men, back in 1977, when Joanne was just six years old. Perhaps this example inspired her! She won the British title for the first time when she was just 15. By the time she was 21, she had won it four times. If she can stay clear of injury, who says she won't break that 40-year duck?

STUART McCALL If you are born in Yorkshire it is most likely that your chosen sport will be cricket and that your chosen country will be England. Stuart played cricket as a youngster, but he was not destined to follow in the footsteps of Sir Len Hutton or even Jim Laker. Instead, Stuart opted for football and to emulate the Leeds United stars of the 1970s, such as Billy Bremner and Joe Jordan, who played for Scotland.

☆ IAN'S TEAM ☆

PETER ELLIOTT burst onto the athletics scene when he became the first man for eight years to beat fellow Yorkshireman Seb Coe over 1500m in competition. Peter had spent so much time in the shadow of Seb, Steve Ovett and Steve Cram that this win added confidence to the belief that a working joiner from a British Steel plant at Rotherham could get to the very top and stay there. In 1987 he won a world championship silver in the 800m. Three years later he brought home from Auckland the Commonwealth Games gold at 1500m.

NICK SKELTON This son of a Warwickshire chemist wanted as a youngster to become a National Hunt jockey. A summer spent at Ted Edgar's yard changed his mind and started a relationship that would last twelve years. In 1978, when he was 21, Nick piloted the suitably named Lastic over 7ft 7.25in at Olympia and into the record books, breaking the 41-year-old British high jump record.

GAME 13
Pictureboard

1

2

3

4

GAME 13
Home & Away

JOANNE
Only one Briton has won the Olympic, World and European figure skating titles in the same year. Who is he?

PETER
Name the British athlete who won the silver medal in the 800m at the European Championship in Split, finishing behind Tom McKean.

STUART
Which England international played twice against Everton in FA Cup finals, for different sides, during the 1980s?

NICK
Which German rider won three successive European titles during the 1980s?

BILL
Who captained Ireland on a record 24 occasions between 1963 and 1974?

IAN
Name the first class umpire who scored a century on his Test debut for England as a player.

Eventing: Name the only man in history to have won Badminton on four occasions.

Soccer: Two brothers hit the headlines during the 1990 World Cup Finals, one for being sent off, the other for scoring the winning goal against the defending champions. Which country did they represent?

Horseracing: On Boxing Day 1990 Desert Orchid won a record-breaking fourth King George Sixth Chase. Which course stages this event?

Cycling: What colours are worn by the 'King of the Mountains' during the Tour de France?

Boxing: Who defeated Ronnie Carroll in November 1990 to become the first man in history to retain the British bantamweight title on four successive occasions?

The Senators and the Lightning will be joining the National Ice Hockey League this season. Which two North American cities do they represent?

One-Minute Round

 ☆ **BILL'S TEAM** ☆

1 (1 pt)　Soccer: Who was Britain's first million pound goalkeeper?

2 (1 pt)　Snooker: Who did Steve Davis defeat to win his first world championship final?

3 (2 pts)　Tennis: What is the nationality of Andres Gomes, the 1990 French Open singles champion?

4 (1 pt)　Showjumping: Who won a Hickstead Derby on Vital?

5 (1 pt)　Horseracing: Name the jockey who rode Quest for Fame to a Derby victory.

6 (3 pts)　The following missing names are all famous screen dogs:
　　a) Soccer: Fraser (?)
　　b) Athletics: (?) Viren
　　c) Boxing: (?) Camacho

1 (1 pt) Athletics: Who won both the AAA and UK 1500 metres titles in 1990?

2 (1 pt) Motor racing: In which country did Niki Lauda win his last grand prix victory?

3 (2 pts) Which world championship did Bradford host in 1989?

4 (1 pt) Ice skating: Name the American who won the women's world title in 1986.

5 (1 pt) Soccer: Only one team has won the UEFA Cup three times. Who are they?

6 (3 pts) The missing names are all famous cartoon cats:
a) Cricket: (?) Sobers.
b) Boxing: (?) Mittee.
c) Soccer: (?) Magath.

GAME 13
Mystery Personality

GAME 13 ANSWERS

PICTUREBOARD

1 **Graeme Hick:** Going out to bat v West Indies, Nottingham, 1991.
2 **Wendy Wyland:** US diving champion.
3 **Antonio Pettigrew:** World Champion 400m runner.
4 **Monica Seles:** In action at Flushing Meadow, New York, 1991.

HOME & AWAY

JOANNE (HOME)
John Curry. Curry achieved this hat-trick in 1976. He won the Olympic title in Innsbruck, the World title in Gothenburg and the European title in Geneva.

(AWAY)
Mark Phillips, in 1971, 1972, 1974 and 1981.

PETER (HOME)
David Sharpe. The Jarrow runner's time was 1 min 45.59 sec. The bronze was won by Piotr Pierkarski of Poland.

(AWAY)
Cameroon. Kana Biyik was sent off and Omam Biyik scored the only goal of the match in Argentina's first match of the 1990 World Cup Finals. It was one of only two defeats inflicted on the defending champions in the tournament.

STUART (HOME)
John Barnes. He played for Watford in 1984 (Everton winning 2–0) and for Liverpool in 1989 (Liverpool winning 3–2 after extra time).

(AWAY)
Kempton Park. Desert Orchid was beaten in this race in 1987, by Nupsala, and on his last outing on Boxing Day 1991 when he suffered a crashing fall three fences from home.

NICK (HOME)
Paul Schockemohle. All three titles were won on the same horse, Deister.

(AWAY)
Red and white (polka-dots). Frederico Bahamontes of Spain and Lucien Van Impe of Belgium each won the jersey a record six times.

BILL (HOME)
Tom Kiernan. Ireland's most capped full-back (54 caps) made his debut in 1960. His nephew Michael Kiernan is Ireland's all-time record scorer, with over 300 points to his name.

(AWAY)
Billy Hardy.

IAN (HOME)
Jackie Hampshire, of Yorkshire and Derbyshire. He made his Test debut in 1969 against the West Indies at Lord's, scoring 107. He played for England in eight Tests between 1969 and 1975.

(AWAY)
Ottawa and Tampa respectively. For the 1992–93 season the League will be increased to 24 clubs.

ONE-MINUTE ROUND

BILL'S TEAM
1 Nigel Martyn of Crystal Palace.
2 Doug Mountjoy.
3 Ecuadorian.
4 Joe Turi.
5 Pat Eddery.
6 a) Digby   b) Lasse   c) Hector.

IAN'S TEAM
1 Neil Horsfield of Newport.
2 Holland (Zandvoort).
3 Speedway.
4 Debbie Thomas.
5 Barcelona, in 1958, 1960 and 1966.
6 a) Garfield   b) Sylvester   c) Felix.

MYSTERY PERSONALITY

BILL'S TEAM   Sally Gunnell: UK 400m hurdler.

IAN'S TEAM   Wasim Akram: Lancashire and Pakistan pace bowler.

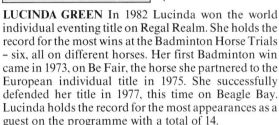

GAME 14

Ian is joined by eventer Lucinda Green and Ryder Cup golfer
Mark James. Scotland's Tom McKean joins the Manchester
United and England midfielder Neil Webb in Bill's team.

✡ IAN'S TEAM ✡

LUCINDA GREEN In 1982 Lucinda won the world
individual eventing title on Regal Realm. She holds the
record for the most wins at the Badminton Horse Trials
– six, all on different horses. Her first Badminton win
came in 1973, on Be Fair, the horse she partnered to the
European individual title in 1975. She successfully
defended her title in 1977, this time on Beagle Bay.
Lucinda holds the record for the most appearances as a
guest on the programme with a total of 14.

MARK JAMES first made the headlines when he
finished as the leading British golfer in the 1976 Open
at Royal Birkdale, a feat he would repeat in 1979. Mark
has played in the Ryder Cup on five occasions and
represented England in the World Cup seven times. In
1990 Mark won two major televised events in England,
the Dunhill British Masters and the NM English Open.

✡ BILL'S TEAM ✡

TOM McKEAN Tom was so full of nerves on his first
appearance in the show that if David Coleman had
asked him to spell his name the opposition would have
got the points! Well, perhaps not quite. Tom printed his
name in the record books by winning the silver medal
in the 800m at the World Championships in 1987.
Three years later he won the 800m in the World Indoor
Championships in Glasgow.

NEIL WEBB The Manchester United and England
midfielder made his football League debut with Reading in 1980. After a three-year spell at Portsmouth he
moved on to Nottingham Forest. Neil made his England debut in 1987 – and history by becoming the
1000th player to be capped for England. During his
spell with Manchester United the club has won the FA
Cup and the European Cup Winners' Cup.

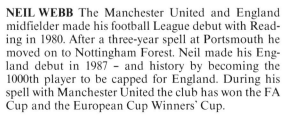

Pictureboard

1

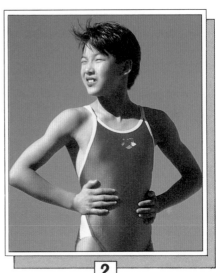

2

3

4

?

GAME 14
Home & Away

LUCINDA
Name the only horse to win Badminton twice in the 1980s.

TOM
Britain's Peter Elliott finished fourth in the Olympic 800m final in Seoul, the highest placed European runner. Can you name the winner?

MARK
Which course staged the Ryder Cup in Britain prior to the Belfry?

NEIL
Which member of Crystal Palace's FA Cup final team in 1990 had already won an FA Cup medal with Wimbledon?

IAN
Which player was released by his county in 1990 despite scoring seven first class centuries and finishing third in the batting averages?

BILL
J.P.R. Williams is one of only three players whose international career spanned the 1960s, 1970s and 1980s. Who are the other two?

Cycling: Which colour jersey does the Tour de France's most consistent rider have the right to wear?

In which sport is it possible to shoot a Snowman in the Desert?

Roger Yves Bost and Norton de Rhuys were members of the French team that won the World Team Championship in 1990. What was the sport?

In what sport might you be called an Aunt Emma if you weren't prepared to Dolly Rush?

Soccer: Name the England goalkeeper who played in five FA Cup finals between 1971 and 1987.

In which sport would infringing the 'five-minute rule' result in disqualification?

One-Minute Round

 IAN'S TEAM

1 (1 pt) Horseracing: What is the youngest age at which a horse can run in the Grand National?

2 (1 pt) Swimming: At which event did Norbert Rozsa win a European Championship title?

3 (2 pts) Golf: Who has won the British Open most times?

4 (1 pt) Eventing: Name the New Zealander who took the world title in Stockholm.

5 (1 pt) Tennis: Only one man has won the French Open title six times. Who is he?

6 (3 pts) You might find the following missing names around a fireplace:
   a) Cricket: Trevor (?)
   b) Tennis: Arthur (?)
   c) Golf: Bobby (?)

BILL'S TEAM

1 (1 pt) Athletics: Who is the reigning Commonwealth champion at 400m?

2 (1 pt) At which sport is Matthew Pinsent a world champion?

3 (2 pts) Soccer: Who scored the winner for Nottingham Forest in the 1990 League Cup final?

4 (1 pt) Motorcycling: The 1990 World Champion Wayne Rainey failed to finish in only one grand prix that year. Name it.

5 (1 pt) Tennis: Which Australian ended Boris Becker's two-year unbeaten run at Wimbledon in 1987?

6 (3 pts) Their missing surnames are all found in Westerns:
a) Cricket: Malcolm (?)
b) Soccer: Derek(?)
c) Canoeing: Andrew (?)

117

GAME 14
Mystery Personality

☆ IAN'S TEAM ☆

☆ BILL'S TEAM ☆

GAME 14 ANSWERS

PICTUREBOARD

1 **Sharon Rendle:** World featherweight judo champion in 1987 and 1989.
2 **Minxia Fu:** China's 3-metre platform diving World Champion.
3 **Kenny Harrison:** US triple jumper.
4 **Sachin Tendulkar:** Indian cricket prodigy.

HOME & AWAY

LUCINDA (HOME)
Sir Wattie, ridden by Ian Stark. This partnership won Badminton in 1986 and 1988. Lucinda has won six Badminton titles since 1973.

(AWAY)
Green. Points are awarded to the first 25 finishers in each stage of the race. The yellow jersey is the second most important award of the Tour.

TOM (HOME)
Paul Ereng of Kenya. The silver went to the 1984 champion, Joachim Cruz, and the bronze to Said Aouita.

(AWAY)
Golf. A Snowman is a triple bogey. The Desert is the fourteenth at Sawgrass, the home of the TPC and the headquarters of the US PGA.

MARK (HOME)
Walton Heath, in 1981. The Ryder Cup competition first came to the Belfry in 1985. Europe won for the first time since 1957.

(AWAY)
Showjumping. Roger Yves Bost and Norton de Rhuys were one of the partnerships in the team of four which won the team gold. The others were Eric Navet riding Malesan Quito de Baussy – who also took the individual title, Hubert Bourdy riding Morgat and Pierre Durand on Jappeloup. The championships were held in Stockholm.

NEIL (HOME)
Andy Thorn. He was in the Wimbledon side that beat Liverpool 1–0 in the 1988 final.

(AWAY)
Croquet. An Aunt Emma is the name given to a player who makes little attempt to set up breaks. A Dolly Rush is a rush in which the two balls are very close together.

IAN (HOME)
Tom Moody. His average of 89.46, for Warwickshire, was bettered only by Graham Gooch and Graeme Hick. Warwickshire decided to keep Alan Donald as the overseas player, releasing Moody who has since joined Worcestershire.

(AWAY)
Ray Clemence with Liverpool – in 1971 v Arsenal (lost); in 1974 v Newcastle (won); in 1977 v Manchester United (lost). With Spurs – in 1982 v QPR (won) and in 1987 v Coventry (lost).

BILL (HOME)
John Hipwell, Australian scrum-half, who won 36 caps between 1968 and 1982, and Nigel Horton (England), who won 20 caps between 1969 and 1980. J.P.R. Williams (Wales) won 55 caps between 1969 and 1981.

(AWAY)
Yachting. Any boat that crosses the starting line in the five minutes before the off is disqualified.

ONE-MINUTE ROUND

IAN'S TEAM
1 Seven.
2 100m Breaststroke.
3 Harry Vardon, six times.
4 Blyth Tait, on Messiah in 1990.
5 Bjorn Borg.
6 a) Gard   b) Ashe   c) Cole.

BILL'S TEAM
1 Darren Clark of Australia.
2 Rowing; he partnered Steven Redgrave in the coxless pairs.
3 Nigel Jemson.
4 The Hungarian, in Budapest in September.
5 Peter Doohan.
6 a) Marshall   b) Posse   c) Sheriff.

MYSTERY PERSONALITY

IAN'S TEAM   Craig McDermott: Australian pace bowler.

BILL'S TEAM   A.J. Kitt: US downhill skier.

GAME 15

In this final game Bill's guests are cricketer Devon Malcolm and footballing Irishman Niall Quinn. Scotland's golfer Sam Torrance joins athlete Tessa Sanderson with Ian whose hopes of a win are high.

☆ BILL'S TEAM ☆

DEVON MALCOLM Born in Kingston, Jamaica, in 1963, Devon made his first-class debut in 1984. He won his first Test match cap five years later, in 1989, against Australia at Trent Bridge. The following winter he toured the West Indies and in the Third Test he became the first English bowler since Tony Greig (1974–75) to take ten wickets in a Test match against the West Indies on their own soil.

NIALL QUINN The Manchester City and Republic of Ireland striker was born in Dublin in 1966. He began his soccer career with Arsenal, and on his League debut in December 1985 immediately joined the ranks of a very elite band by scoring against Liverpool. In 1987 he won a League Cup winners medal, Arsenal defeating Liverpool in the final. In March 1990 he moved to Maine Road for a fee of £800,000. Niall made his international debut in 1986 against Iceland. He was a member of Ireland's European championship squad in 1988 and their World Cup squad in 1990.

☆ IAN'S TEAM ☆

SAM TORRANCE will always be remembered as the man who sank the putt that gave Europe their first Ryder Cup victory. Sam relaxes from the pressures of the golf course by playing snooker and tennis, but it was in his snooker room standing on the table listening to Dire Straits that he overcame a problem with his putting and invented that long-shafted putter for which he is now famous.

TESSA SANDERSON won an Olympic gold medal for the javelin at the 1984 Games in Los Angeles and became the first British athlete to win a throwing event in the history of the Olympics. She also became the first *A Question of Sport* contestant in twenty-one years to answer a question for the opposite team, when she shouted out an answer during the One-Minute Round. Tessa, who won an unprecedented third Commonwealth Games title at Auckland, likes to relax playing squash or lawn tennis.

121

1

2

3

4

?

GAME 15
Home & Away

DEVON
Who was the leading wicket-taker in the 1990–91 Test series between Australia and England?

SAM
Name the two golfers who have each won the German Open four times since 1980.

NIALL
Which Scottish international played in four FA Cup finals for Everton in the 1980s?

TESSA
In 1932 Mildred Didrickson of the United States became the first non-European to win an Olympic javelin title. Who became the second in 1980?

BILL
Name the last man to play international rugby and Test cricket for England.

IAN
Who took four West Indies Test wickets in five balls in December 1990?

In which sport has Britain's Steve Webster been world champion four times?

Who was the first English-speaking winner of the Tour de France?

Name the unranked player who reached the semi-finals of the 1990 UK Championship after defeating Jimmy White in the quarter-finals?

Rugby Union: What is the family name of the three brothers who became legends in the 1980s by all winning international caps for their country?

Scotland caused a major upset when they defeated the world team champions England in a fight-off for the United Kingdom grand slam title in Glasgow in December 1990. What was the sport?

Rallying: Name the Finn who has won 19 or more world championship rallies.

One-Minute Round

☆ BILL'S TEAM ☆

1 (1 pt)   Cricket: Who was the leading Test wicket-taker in the 1980s?

2 (1 pt)   Horseracing: Which course stages the Welsh Grand National?

3 (2 pts)   Boxing: At what weight did Paul Hodkinson win a world title?

4 (1 pt)   Soccer: Name the non League side that knocked West Brom out of the 1991 FA Cup.

5 (1 pt)   Tennis: Alexander Volkov ended a 23-match winning streak and whose hopes of a first US Open title in 1990?

6 (3 pts)   The following missing surnames are all types of emotion:
      a) Tennis: Matt (?)
      b) Golf: Orville (?)
      c) Cricket: Jim (?)

1 (1 pt)   Golf: Who did Nick Faldo beat in a play-off to win his first US Masters title?

2 (1 pt)   Boxing: At which weight did Jim Watt hold the world title?

3 (2 pts)   Table tennis: Who was the last British player to win a world title?

4 (1 pt)   Athletics: Name the United Kingdom javelin champion who finished fourth at the Commonwealth Games in Auckland.

5 (1 pt)   Snooker: Which player reached world championship finals in both 1990 and 1991?

6 (3 pts)   The following missing surnames are all European countries:
   a) Showjumping: Jean (?)
   b) Soccer: Geoff (?)
   c) Cricket: Bob (?)

GAME 15
Mystery Personality

☆ IAN'S TEAM ☆

GAME 15 ANSWERS

PICTUREBOARD

1 **Vreni Schneider:** Swiss skiing ace, saluting her victory at Saalbach in 1991.
2 **Steve Waugh:** Australian batsman, relaxing in Saudi Arabia, 1990.
3 **Dalton Grant:** Britain's leading high jumper.
4 **Michael Stich:** Wimbledon Men's Singles Champion, 1991.

HOME & AWAY

DEVON (HOME)
Bruce Reid. He took 27 wickets at an average of 16 runs. Devon took most wickets for England, with 16.

(AWAY)
Motorcycling (Sidecar racing). He was awarded an MBE in 1990, a season in which he finished third in the championship race.

SAM (HOME)
Mark McNulty of Zimbabwe and Bernhard Langer on his home soil. McNulty was victorious in 1980, 1987, 1990 and 1991, while Langer won in 1981, 1982, 1985 and 1986.

(AWAY)
Greg Lemond of the USA. He won it in 1986, ending a five-year run of French victories.

NIALL (HOME)
Graeme Sharp. He was only on the winning side once in 1984 when he scored in Everton's 2–0 win over Watford. Everton lost in 1985 against Manchester United and in 1986 and 1989 against Liverpool.

(AWAY)
Alan McManus. The 19-year-old Scot defeated Dennis Taylor, Steve Newbury and Silvino Francisco to reach the semis. He was defeated by fellow countryman Stephen Hendry, who went on to win the final 16–15 against Steve Davis.

TESSA (HOME)
Maria Colon of Cuba with a throw of 68.40m. Colon also became the first Cuban woman to win an Olympic gold medal.

(AWAY)
Ella (Mark, Glen and Gary). Between them they won 37 caps for Australia between 1980 and 1984.

BILL (HOME)
Mike Smith (M.J.K.). He played
one rugby union international
against Wales in 1956 while he
was at Oxford University. He
played 50 Tests between 1958 and
1972, and captained his country in
25 Tests.

(AWAY)
Karate.

IAN (HOME)
Wasim Akram of Pakistan. Jeff
Dujon, Curtley Ambrose, Malcolm
Marshall and Courtney Walsh
were dismissed by him in the Third
Test in Lahore. He was denied five
out of five when Imran Khan just
failed to catch Ian Bishop. Only
two other men have taken four out
of five, Maurice Allom and Chris
Old, both of England.

(AWAY)
Markku Alen, World Champion
in 1978.

ONE-MINUTE ROUND

BILL'S TEAM
1 Malcolm Marshall, with 323 wickets.
2 Chepstow.
3 Featherweight.
4 Woking.
5 Stefan Edberg.
6 a) Anger   b) Moody   c) Love.

IAN'S TEAM
1 Scott Hoch.
2 Lightweight.
3 Johnny Leach, in 1951.
4 Sharon Gibson.
5 Jimmy White. He was beaten on both occasions.
6 a) Germany   b) Ireland   c) Holland.

MYSTERY PERSONALITY

BILL'S TEAM   Roger Black: European and Commonwealth 400m
champion.

IAN'S TEAM   Mike Atherton: dressed up for the England team's
Christmas party in Melbourne, 1990.